# Jesus Loves Us Even Though

## We Are: Impractical, Impulsive, Impatient... *Imperfect*

Angela Beck Kalnins

Cover Photo
© Can Stock Photo Inc/Kurhan

ISBN-10:
061596916X
ISBN-13:
978-0-615-96916-9

# Dedication

I dedicate this to the ones I love.

Because of you, my family—the ones who've known me the longest and the ones who have just arrived—I found the courage to take a risk and do something I never dreamed I would ever do. So, this is for you, my husband and children, those born to me and those who "opted" in. This is for my parents, *my grandchildren*, my siblings, nieces and nephews, aunts, uncles and cousins; this is for my grandparents—long gone but never forgotten. You have *all* inspired me. Your loving support and your enthusiasm for what I do—*everything I do*—makes it fun to be me!

I love each of you more than I could ever say.


***Lester, you are the love of my life and I thank God for you every day***!


Thanks also go to Lori Kincer—*my favorite sounding board and most honest "red inker"*. You are a true friend.

Thank you, Susan Tolleson. I could not have done it without you—period.

You have been a true blessing to me.

To my friends…Joanie most of all… I love you!

***And, for Lizzie—for whom this all began—***
***Grammy loves you!***

And, above all else, my deepest and most heart-felt gratitude goes to the Good Lord who loves me…even though.

# Contents

*Song of Songs –* When a Man Loves a Woman

*Isaiah –* Twinkle, Twinkle

*Jeremiah –* Cracked Pots

*Lamentations –* When the Rain Falls

*Ezekiel –* It's All About Me…Or, Is It?

*Daniel –* Even If
*Hosea –* Push Me, Pull you

*Joel –* Warning Signs

*Amos –* The Plumb Line

*Obadiah –* To Gloat or Not to Gloat

*Jonah –* A Whale of a Tale

*Micah –* The Bread of Life

*Nahum –* "Daddy You're Mean!"

*Habakkuk –* Reaching for the Light

*Zephaniah –* I'll Call You

*Haggai –* Mea Culpa! Mea Culpa!

*Zechariah –* When You Can't, He Can

*Malachi –* The End of the Rainbow

**New Testament**
*Matthew –* Mountaintop Experiences

*Mark –* All You Need Is Love

*Luke –* Trust and Obey

*John –* Step Out of the Boat

*Acts –* "In the Beginning"

*Romans* – The New Square!

*1 Corinthians* – Sticks and Stones

*2 Corinthians* – Forgive and Forget

*Galatians* – Sole Fide—Faith Alone

*Ephesian* – Only the Strong Survive!

*Philippians* – Called by Name

*Colossians* – The Power of His Name

*1 Thessalonians* – It's Okay to be the "Bad Guy"

*2 Thessalonians* – The Devil Is Coming! The Devil Is Coming!

*1 Timothy* – 20/20 Vision

*2 Timothy* – Their Legacy

*Titus* – In Chains

*Philemon* – It Only Takes a Spark

*Hebrews* – Waiting for an Answer

*James* – Just a Man

*1 Peter* – The King of the Jungle?

*2 Peter* – Liars and Con-Men and Cheats! Oh, My!

*1 John* – Turn Your Eyes Upon Jesus

*2 John* – Anyway

*3 John* – Monkey See, Monkey Do

*Jude* – Crouching Tiger

*Revelation* – The Nature of Worship

*Epilogue* – Even Though

# Prologue

I'm a good person.

I go to church on Sundays, donate to the Salvation Army, eat my broccoli and pay my taxes. I love my family. I get along with my neighbors and I'm kind to strangers. I obey traffic laws (most of them) and vote in every election. And, it must be said I have never kicked a puppy, taken candy from a little one or clubbed a baby seal!

*However*

Everyone makes mistakes.

I know I've made my fair share; I'll admit it. I've broken a commandment (or two), taken the wrong path more than once and I've made bad choices. I've done stupid things and led others astray. I've told myself little white lies are okay and harsh words are only words. I've hurt the ones I love *and* I've yelled at my dog. So, yes…I *have* made mistakes. Who hasn't? I'm only human and…

Nobody's perfect.

There has only ever been one perfect human being and I am certainly not Him. The good news is, I know Him—*personally*—and He loves me! Me!

Jesus loves me even though I'm impractical, impulsive, impatient and imperfect. He loves me even though I'm often clueless and stubborn and sometimes…*really awful*. He loves me, the real me. The truth is…

There is redemption in His love.

There is no selfish act, no wrong choice, no stupid mistake, nor any person on earth—even our own stubborn, reckless, incorrigible selves—who can come between us and the love of Christ! He will always love us…*even though*.

When I started writing with purpose, in 2006, my intention was to create a Faith journal for my newly born granddaughter. I wanted to share with her some of the many heart-stopping, life-changing, eternally significant messages I have received from the Lord through His Word over the years. So, in a small spiral notebook I recorded each important scripture and a note or two about its meaning to me. I wanted Lizzie, my granddaughter, to know that even though none of us is perfect, we can be made perfect *in Him*.

I shared this idea with a friend, a new Christian, and allowed her to read some of the entries in my diary. She began asking questions:

- "I don't get it. Why this scripture?"
- "I don't know anything about 2 Chronicles. What's it about?"
- "This scripture is about 'loving your neighbor' but your notes are about anger. Why?"

So, I shared with her why those particular scriptures were important to me; I told her the stories that set each scripture into context. She asked, "Why didn't you do that to begin with?"

And, with that, this book was born.

Over the years, I've found at least one important message from each of the 66 books of the Bible. I'd like to share them with you. They're in order from Genesis to Revelation. For those of you who may be new to Christianity or the scriptures, like my friend, I've included at the beginning of each story, a small paragraph—call it a synopsis of each Bible Book.

Whether you've read the Bible once, five times or never before, I am hoping you can relate to each scripture I've shared here in some way. There *is* a way to do that. After reading each narrative I'd like to ask you to do a little journaling. Record YOUR thoughts; ask YOUR questions; find YOUR truths. I've provided one or two "starter" questions to prime your journaling machinery; to grease the wheels, so to speak. Use them to get your ball rolling…. or make up some of your own. The only way to find the YOU in this exercise is to do what's best… for <u>you</u>.

You will also find those important scriptures I was telling you about, at the beginning of each story. These are the very scriptures that have touched my life over the years and I hope you see the same thrilling relevancy in them as I did. For the purposes of this book I have taken most of these scriptures from the NIV version of the Bible; although, once or twice, I used other versions. When I have, it is indicated, in parenthesis at the end of reference.

At the end of each story you'll also find a prayer. These are my prayers…but, I'm hoping you'll use them to bring your Spirit in touch with His. Like the journaling questions, they are there for only one purpose…to get *you* started. Read my prayers and let them run into your own or skip them altogether and pray straight from your own heart.

God speaks to us all every day in a million ways; all we have to do, is get in on the conversation. Talk to Him; listen to Him. Follow His advice, answer when He calls and laugh with Him when you mess everything up. That's what I do.

I'm not a perfect human being. I am not a perfect Christian. I mess up every day in more ways than I can ever count. And because of this I've actually had a hard time making the decision to publish this book. After all, I ask myself, *who am I?* Who am I to try to lead anyone through the Bible, to the right path...to God? I'm not a pastor. I'm not a teacher or a leader (though I've been both in the past). I'm a mom and a wife and a grandmother with 30 extra pounds on my frame, gray hair on my head and a Southern accent so thick it often causes others to cringe... I'm a mess. It's true. However, the one message I've received from God over and over again through the years is this: despite it all. Jesus loves me.... *even though.*

He loves you too.

# Genesis

God made the world with love. Genesis is the story of its beginning. It is the story of earth's origin, the birth of man, the rise of civilization, the foundation of faith, the beginning of religion, *and*...the fall of humanity. It is the beginning of our journey back from sin and toward a deeper more personal relationship with God.

# Made with Love

*³Now Israel [Jacob] loved Joseph more than any of his other sons, because he had been born to him in his old age; and he made a richly ornamented robe for him. –Genesis 37:3*

I don't like to think of myself as a perfectionist but the sad truth is that's who I am...sometimes.

One year, for my birthday, my parents presented me with a very special gift–a quilt top my grandmother had pieced together herself. Mother hoped I would use it to make a beautiful completed quilt. *I* hoped my parents would not notice the anxiety on my face, the twitch of my left eyelid, or how my hands shook upon seeing it.

I was appalled by the mismatched seams and oh-so-inelegant stitching which formed dozens of clumsily pieced lop-sided five-pointed stars made from thousands of scraps of incompatible fabric; all these were awkwardly attached to a bright yellow muslin background. I disliked the whole thing on sight.

Mother didn't notice. She became weepy as she began telling the history of the quilt. She told how my grandmother had lovingly pieced it together using fabric from old baby clothes, a bassinette cover, some old kitchen curtains and old bed clothes. She'd begun working on it some twenty (or more) years before. Unfortunately, she passed away before completing it.

Even more unfortunate was my inability to appreciate Grandma's hard work and artistry. Although mother wanted me to complete Grandma's project, my fastidiousness just wouldn't let me. So, I packed it away in the attic and forgot all about it.

Years later while visiting a friend, I found myself amazed by her collection of beautifully well-preserved, handmade, antique quilts. She said, "Let me show you my favorite." From beneath a stack of magazine cover-worthy quilts and duvets, she pulled a coverlet made by *her* grandmother. It looked almost identical to mine!

She lovingly caressed the same faded and frayed yellow muslin background and the same lopsided five-pointed stars made from pieces of old baby clothes and long-gone leisure suits. She explained how her grandmother had found the pattern in a *Women's Day* magazine in 1965. My grandmother must have used the same pattern!

My friend adoringly hugged her quilt to her chest and talked about how much time and how many memories were invested in it. Like mine, hers too was a true perfectionist's nightmare; it was...*ungainly and graceless*. Yet, despite its flaws she loved it, unconditionally, simply because her grandmother had made it.

During my birthday celebration years before, instead of enjoying my mother's enthusiasm for the gift she'd given, I had wasted the moment judgmentally inspecting its frayed edges. Instead of noticing my dad's quiet moment of sentimental reflection, I sat horrified by the crooked stitching and unbalanced stars. Talk about graceless! Suddenly realizing how much my snobbery had cost me, I felt my knees go weak. Shame washed over me in waves. Even now, tears come to my eyes when I think of how horribly I acted.

That afternoon I drove home sobbing like a child. Once there, I dug through the attic until I found the quilt top and began the process of finishing grandma's quilt.

Today, it is one of my most prized possessions. I've come to realize perfection belongs to God alone. It isn't mine to have or achieve. That realization brought to my heart an appreciation for all things made with love, including me.

Aren't we blessed God looks at us as my friend looked at her grandmother's quilt? He doesn't see our flaws and blemishes. He sees us as things of beauty no matter how frayed or lopsided we are. He considers us worthy even though...

Think of the thief who hung on the cross next to Jesus. Some eyes must have seen only a degenerate, amoral, and worthless human being, one deserving of his fate. Yet, through the eyes of love, God saw something different. He looked upon the imperfection of humanity and instead, saw the perfection of His plan. The Lord forgave the thief his blemishes and unworthiness, and ushered him into heaven like a long-lost and much-loved son.

*[43] Jesus answered him, "Truly I tell you, today you will be with me in paradise." —Luke 23:43*

He does the same with you and me! Like Joseph's coat of many colors we, too, were made with love. We shouldn't be ashamed of who we have been. Instead, we must claim who we can be, *in Him.*

We were made with perfect love and we are beautiful!

### PRAYING TOGETHER

*Father God, Abba, I can only be what I am; flawed, defective and inadequate. Show me the true splendor in every person, place and thing before I* *shame myself looking for perfection, instead. I pray Father you will lead me to be more like you to love the saint within the sinner… <u>especially when it's me</u>. Amen.*

### *JOURNALING YOUR THOUGHTS*

Isn't it wonderful how God's love sees past the uneven seams and frayed edges of our lives? Journal your thoughts and feelings on unconditional love with the help of the prompt provided.

What does the term "unconditional love" mean to you? Explain.

# Exodus

The second book of the Bible is called Exodus. Its name comes from the Greek **Exodos**, meaning "going out". It covers a 145-year history of the Hebrew people, following their progress from the beginning of their slavery to their escape from Egypt—their *going out*—and beyond. Within the pages of Exodus, we learn the story of God's gift to them of the Ten Commandments, the basic principles by which we still live today.

# The Cat's Meow

*[3] "You shall have no other gods before me. [4] You shall not make for your self an idol in the form of anything in heaven above or on the earth beneath or in the waters below."* —*Exodus 20:3-4*

What do you think of when you hear the words, *idol worship*? I imagine wooden statues, golden calves and maybe...Tom Cruise. I know some who might think of money or power or even food. The truth is we can make idols of just about anything, even ourselves.

Let me tell you a quick story.

Years ago, when I was young and stupid, I became friends with a very nice man in my office. He was a nice guy and I found it very comfortable to be around him.

However, there came a time when I began to notice he was looking at me differently—as more than just a friend. He began to openly flirt with and flatter me. Because I was a married woman, his attention made me uncomfortable…in the beginning. Yet, I have to admit it; there was something very gratifying about the attention he gave to me. Even as I told myself to put a stop to it, even as I lectured myself on the danger of letting it go too far, I began to revel in his interest.

In all honesty I wasn't attracted to him. I did (and do) love my husband very much. *Yet…*I was enthralled with the idea this other man might be attracted to me! When he flirted, flattered and fawned over me, my self-esteem puffed up like a balloon. For just a little while, I thought I was the cat's meow. In fact, I became so full of myself it is a wonder I didn't collapse under the weight of it all.

As I knew it would, the penultimate moment eventually arrived.

One day, after work, he caught me alone outside of the building and asked me to go for a drink and some "alone time". I declined and reminded him we were both married to others. He argued, good naturedly (at first) and teasingly accused me of leading him on. I gave him the "we should just be friends" speech. It was all so sweetly delivered (and oh-so-rehearsed). I suppose, in my naïveté I had hoped we could just go on as we had been, him worshipping me…but, from afar…and me luxuriating in his adoration.

That isn't what happened, of course.

I was completely caught off guard when he suddenly became incredibly angry and very aggressive, physically pinning me to a wall, screaming into my face. He called me horrible names and said horrendously insulting things.

Frankly, I've never been so frightened. Unfortunately, I had no one to blame but myself. I had become so enamored with the idea of being someone else's object of affection that in a weird kind of way I had begun to idolize myself. I had begun to believe my own hype. I felt I deserved his attention. However, by allowing the attraction to go on, to satisfy my own twisted esteem issues, what had started out (in my mind) as an innocent flirtation had very suddenly become much darker and more terrifying.

By placing myself on a pedestal, by not shutting him down from the first moment I realized how he was feeling, I made myself available to him. It was really no surprise things happened the way they did.

Fortunately, I have been blessed with a wicked right jab. I reacted instinctually, punching him in the nose. I didn't do much physical damage, but the blow was just hard enough to break his hold on me, *completely*.

The rest of the story isn't important. What *is* important is how blessed I feel by the experience, truly. I was forced to face my mistake before it became a much bigger one. Not everyone is given *or takes* that opportunity. Some people get so caught up in the climb to the top of their own pedestal they forget who is *supposed* to be up there.

God detests the things we try to put before Him: wooden idols, golden calves, money, power, possessions—these are all dangerous to our relationship with Him. However, with eyes wide open we can usually see them coming. We can defend against them—*if we choose to*—and we can turn away from their lure. It's the creation of the subtler idols we have to be very aware of and guard against.

Before I allow myself to get wrapped up in the glory of me again, I have to remember it is God who created the world from nothing. It is God who forged humanity from a single man. It is God who performed miracles, bringing sight to the blind, making the lame to walk, bringing the dead to life. It is God who sacrificed a living Son for the sins of man. It is God who deserves the glory.

God is the only being truly worthy of my worship—and yours.

*He* is the Cat's Meow!

### PRAYING TOGETHER

*Father, awesome God, creator of everything, I worship you and you alone. Lead me in your ways and keep me from traveling down any road that would take me into idol worship of anything or anyone, especially of myself! I pray these things, Father, because I want to follow your commands. I want to be faithful to you alone and live obediently before you! I pray in the name of Jesus Christ. Amen.*

### JOURNALING YOUR THOUGHTS

Idol worship is often more insidious than bowing down before golden calves. When we allow our attention to be taken from God and focused elsewhere we are participating in the worship of idols. Take some time to evaluate your focus.

Have I ever allowed myself to lose focus on God by idolizing something or someone else? Explain

# Leviticus

Taking its name from the tribe of Levi, God's chosen priests; the book of Leviticus is an outline of God's laws. This book describes the proper procedures for making offerings and sacrifices; it outlines the duties of the priests; summarizes dietary and medical laws, holidays, rituals and ethics; and Leviticus defines the need for God's laws in the first place. It places value on trusting in Him. The book of Leviticus is the quintessential guidebook to those who find themselves in the pursuit of holiness.

# The Pursuit of Holiness

*37 " Keep all my decrees and all my laws and follow them. I am the LORD." —Leviticus 19:37*

I have to confess something. I am a reality TV show junkie. I love shows like *Survivor*, *American Idol, and Top Chef.* But, one of my favorites is *Big Brother*.

The premise of *Big Brother* is simple: Place a group of twelve strangers in one house with only three bedrooms and one bathroom and ask them to live together 24/7 for twelve weeks, while being constantly filmed. Throw in a few competitions resulting in rewards and/or punishments; add a controversy or two; ask the houseguests to vote each other out of the house one by one (until the last one standing wins it all) and let the viewers sit back and watch what happens.

The "showmances" are always fun and the friendships created and destroyed (sometimes all in one episode) are captivating; I also find the manipulations, schemes and plots engrossing. What I don't find much of, while watching *Big Brother,* is holiness. Even the contestants who claim to be Christians in the first few days of filming are often, by the end of the season, just as rakish, rude and unsavory as everyone else. Let's face it, true holiness just doesn't make for good TV.

One day I came across this headline on an internet news website: ***Israeli* Big Brother *shuts down for Yom Kippur.*** As a true *Big Brother* fan, I had to read more.

In October of 2008, when all of Israel went still to mark the advent of the most solemn of all Jewish celebrations, Yom Kippur, the Israeli *Big Brother* producers did something they've never before done on the show. They constructed a temporary Jewish synagogue for their one religious contestant and stopped production for the High Holy holiday.

Asher Simoni, a 29-year-old Israeli postal clerk and devoted Jew, had already turned the Israeli *Big Brother* set on its ear, even before the start of Yom Kippur. Because of him, *Big Brother* and its houseguests were observing Jewish dietary laws from day one. For instance, non-kosher meat was never served—goat, pork, shellfish or lobster— nor was meat ever mixed with dairy in the Israeli *Big Brother* kitchen. Never before had the show's producers made such concessions for any contestant.

There were other special considerations to make. Orthodox Jewish law requires men to pray daily during Yom Kippur and to do so in groups of ten which are known as "minyan." Since there were no other Jewish participants on the show or among the crew, the producer brought in nine Jewish volunteers, every day, to pray with Simoni in the temporary synagogue constructed adjacent the *Big Brother* house.

I know very little about Yom Kippur (only what I've researched and recorded here) but, as a huge fan of *Big Brother*, I know this singular show of faith and holiness on the part of a contestant like Mr. Simoni is awe-inspiring. At least, it is for me.

It would have been very easy for the contestant to shrug his shoulders and say, "Can't be holy now—I'm on TV." But, he didn't. It would have been just as easy—*easier still*—for the show's producers to turn away Mr. Simoni as a contestant, in the first place. Especially when they realized what actions might be necessary to help him live out his religious practices during the show's taping. They didn't. For these reasons, I admire both the contestant and the show.

Christians aren't perfect, but like Mr. Simoni, we **can** be holy.

Holiness is both a state of mind and a way of living. It is the conscious act of worshiping God in every circumstance—in our own bedrooms or on public TV. It is the daily study of scripture and application of those lessons to our lives. It is our supplication to God in good times and bad. It is listening for and following the Spirit of the Lord always, and holiness is putting our selves in the position of acting as examples to others.

Peter said,

*[13] "Therefore, prepare your minds for action; be self-controlled; set your hope fully on the grace to be given you when Jesus Christ is revealed. [14]As obedient children do not conform to the evil desires you had when you lived in ignorance. [15]But just as he who called you is holy, so be holy in all you do; for it is written: 'Be holy, because I am holy.'"*
*—1 Peter 1: 13-16*

If that's a little too intimidating for you (as it was for me), remember this too:

*[13] "I can do all things through Him who strengthens me." –Philippians 4:13*

You may never find yourself on TV. However, you should keep in mind, someone is always watching. Keep your thoughts focused on the one who is always holy and pursue holiness and you will be holy, too!

### PRAYING TOGETHER

*Father in heaven, you are above all things. Still you are close to us and for that, I am grateful. Lead my footsteps with the light of your Word and make me follow you down a different path. Keep me from thinking, saying, and doing those things that would shame you. Make me righteous in your sight, oh Lord. In the name of your Son, Jesus Christ, I pray. Amen.*

### JOURNALING YOUR THOUGHTS

To be holy, set apart and sanctified, can be somewhat hard to do in today's secular world. Explore your thoughts and feelings on the subject by journaling about what pursuing holiness means to you. Use some or all of the prompts provided to help you get started in your journaling:

My definition of holiness is:

Leviticus 20:26 says, *"You must be holy because I, the Lord, am holy…"* How can I set myself apart from others?

# Numbers

Although this book does include a census of the
people it really has very little to do with actual
numbers. Instead, it tells the story of the Israelites'
journey from Mt. Sinai—where they received the
Ten Commandments—to the edge of the land of
Canaan, the Promised Land. Because the people did
not trust God as they should have and turned against
His will, because their leaders became prideful and
too full of themselves, God would not allow any of
them to enter the land of milk & honey. Even the
great leader, Moses, falls prey to temptation in this
book.

# Follow the Leader

*[10]He and Aaron gathered the assembly together in
front of the rock and Moses said to them, "Listen,
you rebels, must we bring you water out of this
rock?" [11]Then Moses raised his arm and struck the
rock twice with his staff. Water gushed out, and the
community and their livestock drank. [12]But the
LORD said to Moses and Aaron, "Because you did*

*not trust in me enough to honor me as holy in the sight of the Israelites, you will not bring this community into the land I give them."*
—Numbers 20:10-12

I'd been sitting on the couch pretending to read a book when, in reality, I was watching my children play "follow the leader." Katie, my oldest, had been the leader for a while and had asked her siblings to do somersaults, jumping jacks, and deep knee-bends. She'd also asked them to walk backwards, skip around the couch until they couldn't catch their breath, and do the fireman's roll.

Baylie, my youngest, was only three and didn't quite understand the object of the game. She was okay with following but had no real desire to lead. So when Katie told Baylie it was her turn to lead, Baylie stuck her thumb in her mouth, plopped down in the middle of the living room floor, and began to cry. She didn't like the idea of her siblings "copying" her. Even after Katie explained the rules several times, Baylie still refused to take on the role of "leader." She didn't want to be out in front, but was just content to be a part of the crowd.

Unfortunately, by the time it was Jonathan's turn to be the one in charge; the girls were just about played out. When Jonathan asked his sisters to crawl on their hands and knees under the kitchen table, Katie went around it instead and Baylie did the duck walk instead of crawling. Jonathan cried out, "You have to do what I say! Mama, make them play right!" Before I could say a single word, Katie announced that she wasn't playing anymore, and wanted to read instead. Then, both girls turned their backs to their brother.

Jonathan turned his soulful brown eyes on me and burst into tears. "They never play right when it's my turn. No one ever lets me be the leader!" I held out my arms as he jumped up on the couch and buried his face in my lap. At eight, Jonathan was learning two very painful lessons: girls can be mean and it's hard to be a leader.

I've been a leader in one form or another since I was a teenager. With decades of leadership experience under my belt, I should be good at it. Some days I am, but other days, not so much. The older I get, the harder it gets. I sometimes find myself becoming increasingly impatient with others. Inside my head I can hear this little voice (sounding an awful lot like my own) shouting, "You have to do what I tell you to do!" My greatest fear is that the little voice will escape the confines of my skull and shout loudly where everyone can hear.

However, leaders don't stomp and yell like babies—*not the good ones, anyway*. Although some people are born with innate leadership qualities, effective leadership is a skill that needs to be practiced and perfected over time. Leaders have to learn to walk a very fine line between assertiveness and kindness. They have to balance power with persuasion. Leaders must learn the difference between dragging their followers where they don't want to go and leading them to where they need to be.

Leadership is a tough job, and not everyone can—or wants—to do it. It's a learned process. For me, the first step was realizing I wasn't really in charge anyway. God is the only one with any real power to change hearts and motivate action.

My own mentor once said to me, "God has placed you in a leadership role. But, remember, your job is to work in accordance with HIS command. He will work *through* you. He doesn't work *for* you." That's been one of the hardest lessons I've had to learn, and am continuing to learn to this day. *My* plans for *my* ministry are secondary to His plans—*period*.

If others follow you, remember *you* should be following God.

### PRAYING TOGETHER

*Father, how blessed I am to be given the responsibility and trust to lead your people. You have placed me in a position not of power but of humility. To lead, I must remember I am led. I ask you to help me restrain my ego and replace it with your will. I ask these things, Father, because I want to do what you would have me do to further your Kingdom and expand your territory. I ask in the name of your son, Jesus Christ. Amen.*

### *JOURNALING YOUR THOUGHTS*

The ability to be a leader is a blessing God only bestows on a few. With leadership comes great responsibility *to follow the Lord.* Are you a leader? Do you have a leader you admire? Today, explore your thoughts and feelings about the gift of leadership.

Do you hold a position of leadership in any area of your life?

Write about it.

Do you depend on God's will and plan to guide your footsteps as you lead?

Why or why not?

Not everyone is given the gift of leadership. If you have been touched by God to lead in His service, the best way to lead is to get out of His way.

# Deuteronomy

Like many of the great leaders of today, Moses
wrote his last memoir as he left office. He called it
Deuteronomy. It is a collection of his finest
speeches, a detailed list of his last actions as the
leader of the Israelite nation and, it includes a
narrative about his last appointment of Joshua as the
new leader of Israel. After Moses led his people in
one last worship service for God and bestowed his
final blessing on them, he climbed the mountain of
Moab, where he had a spectacular view of the
Promised Land, and he lay down and died.

# The View from the Mountain

*⁵And Moses the servant of the LORD died there in
Moab, as the LORD had said.*
*—Deuteronomy 34:5*

"Come here. I want to show you
something." I dragged Lester, my husband, over to
the kitchen table and proudly displayed the two just-
completed scrapbook pages depicting and

celebrating our granddaughter Lizzie's first steps.
He nodded his head in appreciation and then asked,
"Aren't you a little behind? You know, she just
turned four."

"Yes, I know." I waved my hand
distractedly, "I've been very busy."

I tipped my head toward the other end of the
dining room table where my sewing machine sat,
indicating the *incomplete* quilt still beneath the
needle. It had been there for months. Lester said,
"Okay. Let me show *you* something." He grabbed
my elbow and walked me out to the garage where
my "work center" was located.

On the top of my work table was another
quilt—half finished. There was also an embroidery
hoop sitting nearby holding an incomplete cross-
stitched work. Some day, I hoped, it would be a
pillowcase for Lizzie—I started it before she was
born. Hidden beneath the edge of the future
pillowcase was the beginning of a crocheted afghan.
Nearby was a pile of items to be mended. Although,
I've never touched them, I refuse to get rid of them
because, when I have time, I *will* fix them. *Yeah,
right!* There is a shirt at the bottom of the pile that

needs a button. Lester wore it on our honeymoon and we've been married thirty-one years! "You have got to stop with the projects—unless you're going to finish at least one," he insisted walking back into the house, shaking his head.

He's right, of course. I have a terrible habit of starting things and not following through. I'm not alone. Take Moses, for example. Moses wasn't allowed to finish the one project he'd devoted forty years of his life to—getting the Hebrews into the Promised Land.

Just a few miles from the Jordan, with the finish line in sight, God said, *"No, you cannot go."* How tempting it must have been for Moses to pull up the hem of his garment and make a mad dash for the shores on the other side! How he must have wanted to wade through the waters and touch that distant beach, even if just for a moment. To have dreamed for so long, worked so hard, suffered *so much* and still be denied at the very end; heartbreaking. *And yet…* the realization of a dream does not always have to be *lived* to be seen.

The night before he died, Martin Luther King, Jr. said the last words he'd ever say in public:

*"...but it really doesn't matter for me now—because I've been to the mountaintop. Like anybody, I would like to live a long life.... but, I'm not concerned about that now. I just want to do God's will. And He's allowed me to go up to the mountain. And I've looked over. And I've seen the Promised Land. And I may not get there with you. But I want you to know tonight that we as a people will get to the Promised Land. So I'm happy tonight. I'm not worried about anything. I do not fear any man. Mine eyes have seen the glory of the coming of the Lord!"*

Did he know? Did God say to King, *"No, you cannot go"*?

Martin Luther King, Jr. and Moses were both left behind as their people moved forward into a new world and a new life. Their people crossed that river and reached the other side. Yet, neither the Israelites nor the African-Americans of the 1960s would have reached their Promised Land without the help of their leaders—those servants of God.

The very nature of servant-hood is sacrifice. We may all have projects we may never complete; some fulfillments will be beyond our reach. However, when we are obedient to God, when we follow His call, others are able to cross to their own Jordan and reach *their* Promised Land—with or without us. As servants of God, it must be within us to do our part to help make it so.

Our dreams and ambitions may not always be in line with God's will. But God's will is always in line with what's best, with what brings glory to His name. If you find yourself looking at your personal Promised Land from the top of a mountain and not the shore of the Jordan, don't lose hope. Remember Moses? He didn't cross into the Promised Land but he did go straight to Heaven. Sometimes the rewards for sacrifice are greater than what we sacrificed in the first place. And, the view from the mountain is always spectacular!

### PRAYING TOGETHER

*Dear God, how wonderful it must have been to be Moses! To have your ear, your heart and your friendship—he was truly blessed. Though he was not allowed to touch his sandal to the shore of the Promised Land, he was not neglected. You showered him with glory and took him home to be in your presence for eternity! God, I want to be like Moses. I want to be your servant. Lead my footsteps and guide my thoughts toward complete faithfulness, Father. I ask these things, for I know you to be merciful. In Jesus' name, I pray. Amen.*

### *JOURNALING YOUR THOUGHTS*

Do you have a dream? Is there something you'd like to accomplish for God? Are you worried you will never see the end of that goal? Would you spend some time today thinking about that goal and what's holding you back? Write in your journal about your hopes, dreams and even your fears.

My dream is to

_____.

The fear holding me back is

_____.

Is my dream in line with God's will?

# Joshua

Though he began his life as a simple slave in Egypt, upon the death of Moses, Joshua became the leader of a nation. This book tells of his campaign to win the land of Canaan—with God's help—for *and with* the people of Israel. Following God's instruction, Joshua then divided the land between the twelve tribes of Israel. His story is one of success because he truly and faithfully followed the Lord.

# Down by the Riverside

*¹⁴So when the people broke camp to cross the Jordan, the priests carrying the Ark of the Covenant went ahead of them. ¹⁵Now the Jordan is at flood stage all during harvest. Yet as soon as the priests who carried the ark reached the Jordan and their feet touched the water's edge, ¹⁶the water from upstream stopped flowing. It piled up in a heap a great distance away, at a town called Adam in the vicinity of Zarethan, while the water flowing down to the Sea of the Arabah (that is, the Dead Sea) was*

*completely cut off. So the people crossed over*
*opposite Jericho.* —*Joshua 3: 14-16*

Imagine it. You are right there on the bank
of the Jordan River among the people of Israel.
Close your eyes and feel the warm and calming sun
on your face. A slight breeze ruffles your hair and
tickles your eyelashes. Beneath your feet you can
feel sand, tiny pebbles, and the occasional small
shell. From behind you, a camel snorts and stomps
his enormous foot. He shakes his head and his
harness jangles. Somewhere nearby, an ox answers
in kind, moaning softly, and then a donkey brays.
Even the animals are anxious.

There are people around you as far as your
eye can see. Old and young people, men and
women, children and babies…all are standing on
the precipice of a new life. You look down. In your
hands are the hands of your own children—a boy
and a girl. She is little; joyfully jumping from foot
to foot as she waits for you to signal her to move
forward. She looks up and sees you watching her,
and smiles. The boy intently watches all the things
around him. He stands on tiptoe and points at the

priests farther ahead, closer to the water. "Look, Mother!" He is excited, and so are you.

Your eyes follow your little boy's pointing finger and watch, with anticipation, as one by one the priests step into the river. Here the water is at least chest-high and even higher in some places. You gasp in surprise as the deluge suddenly begins to fall away. With every step the priests take, the water level lowers, the flow slows and then, before your very eyes, *it stops*!

The priests cross the muddy floor of the Jordan River, holding the Ark of the Covenant high, singing praises, and worshipping God! Music begins to play; tambourines, lutes, lyres and voices raise together to lift praises to God, and then… Joshua blows the horn—the signal! The time has come! One tentative step at a time, you move from the banks of the Jordan holding your boy back as he longs to rush ahead. You pull your girl forward and she skips slowly behind, lost to a joyful place of her own. You all move to the other side of the riverbed, and into your new life. God is so good!

For forty years the people of Israel wandered in the desert. A whole generation had

passed away—forbidden from entering the
Promised Land because they had lost their faith.
Moses, the leader they followed for decades, was
the last to pass on. A new generation with a new
leader stood on the banks of the river and watched it
go dry just as God had promised it would.

*8 Tell the priests who carry the Ark of the Covenant:*
*'When you reach the edge of the Jordan's waters,*
*go and stand in the river.' 9 Joshua said to the*
*Israelites, "Come here and listen to the words of the*
*LORD your God."*
*11 "See, the ark of the covenant of the Lord of all the*
*earth will go into the Jordan ahead of you. 12 Now*
*then, choose twelve men from the tribes of Israel,*
*one from each tribe. 13 And as soon as the priests*
*who carry the ark of the LORD—the Lord of all the*
*earth —set foot in the Jordan, its waters flowing*
*downstream will be cut off and stand up in a heap."*
*—Joshua 3: 8-9, 11-13*

The Bible goes on to tell us…

*<sup>15</sup> Now the Jordan is at flood stage all during harvest. Yet as soon as the priests who carried the ark reached the Jordan and their feet touched the water's edge, <sup>16</sup> the water from upstream stopped flowing. It piled up in a heap a great distance away, at a town called Adam in the vicinity of Zarethan, while the water flowing down to the Sea of the Arabah (that is, the Dead Sea) was completely cut off. So the people crossed over opposite Jericho. <sup>17</sup> The priests who carried the ark of the covenant of the LORD stopped in the middle of the Jordan and stood on dry ground, while all Israel passed by until the whole nation had completed the crossing on dry ground. —Joshua 3: 15-17*

God chose a time and a place for this miraculous crossing at which the river would be at its highest. That's when He would part the waters and allow the entire nation of Israel to walk through on dry ground. This brought glory to His name and proved His power to a people who should not have needed proof. The town of Adam was seventeen miles upriver. There the waters of the Jordan backed up to stop the flow downriver where God's people stood. Below where the Israelites were, the waters of the Jordan flowed quickly into the Dead Sea, creating a dry place in between for the passing. The people standing on the banks of the Jordan didn't have a clue what was happening so far upriver in Adam. All they saw was dry land before them....

So many of us look at only what stands before us. We don't see the planning, the detail and work God puts into each moment of our lives— *upriver*—to give us the opportunities to make the right choices. Some people see the muddy river bottom and complain their shoes will get ruined if they cross, so they stop, turn around, and choose to go another way.

Others strip off their shoes and socks and revel in the feel of the mud between their toes as they move from one moment in their lives to another. They are happy in the moment, pleasantly surprised by their good fortune, and are thrilled to take advantage of the good thing "fate" has thrown their way.

Some people look upstream and say, "Thank you God for blocking the waters so I can cross.

These are the believers who have faith in God—whether they can see Him working upstream or not. Which person are you?

### PRAYING TOGETHER

*Father God, Creator of Miracles, how I praise you and worship you! You alone are worthy to be praised! I pray you will open my eyes to your work upstream. Never allow me to take for granted the things you do—out of my sight—that give glory to your name. My life may not be easy. Sometimes I will find myself in water up to my neck or over my head...but I have to ask myself, what did you do—* before that—*to prevent me from going under? How much worse could it have been? Or, in my ignorance did I turn around from the easiest route you provided and go the wrong way? God forgive me my arrogance. I pray in the name of Christ Jesus who saw what was upstream and crossed through his violent future to save my life forever. For this and much more, I am grateful.  Amen*

## *JOURNALING YOUR THOUGHTS*

God puts much effort and planning into your life because He cares. In your journal today, record your feelings about the way God has moved in your life. Ask and answer at least one of the following questions to get started. Then, let your journaling juices flow. Write about whatever flows from your heart.

Can you think of a time when you could tell God was moving in your life? Write about it in your journal.

Did you praise Him and thank Him for His work or, did you live just in the moment enjoying the good fortune that came your way?

# Judges

After the death of Joshua, the people of Israel forgot
all God had done for them and turned from Him and
began worshiping the pagan gods of foreigners
living in the land of Canaan. Angered by the
betrayal of His people, God allowed the Hebrews to
fall under the subjugation of their enemies. They
repented and He rescued them appointing a "judge"
to lead them. After a period of time, however, they
fell away again. Unfortunately, this cycle was
repeated 15 times over the next 480 years. Leaders
of some note during this time were Deborah,
Samson, Samuel and Gideon.

# Dumb and Dumber

*[17]Gideon replied, "If now I have found favor in your
eyes, give me a sign that it is really you talking to
me." —Judges 6:17*

I was preparing a lesson for my monthly
Bible study group when I came across a passage in
the book of Luke that caught my eye. I'm sure I've

read it dozens of times before, yet for the first time it struck me as funny.

*19 And the angel answering said unto him, "I am Gabriel, who stands in the presence of God; and am sent to speak unto thee, and to show thee these glad tidings. 20 And, behold, thou shalt be dumb, and not able to speak, until the day that these things shall be performed, because thou believest not my words, which shall be fulfilled in their season."*
*—Luke 1:19-20 (**KJV**)*

It was the phrase "thou shalt be dumb" that set my giggle box to vibrating. Of course we know when Gabriel used the term "dumb" he meant mute, silent, or unable to speak. But if you think about it, in that moment Zacharias was *acting* kind of dumb—as in ignorant, dense, dimwitted, stupid…etc.

Let's look back a few passages to verse 11 which reads,

*11"And there appeared unto him an angel of the Lord standing on the right side of the altar of incense. (Luke 1:11)."*

Gabriel—**an angel of God**—had just given Zacharias the wonderful news his wife Elizabeth would bear the son he'd always wanted. Instead of jumping for joy, Zacharias asks—in what I hope was only a momentary lapse of intelligence—

*18"How can I be sure of this? I am an old man and my wife is well along in years (Luke1:18 NIV).*

What a stupid question! Let's review…**an angel appeared to him**…

To the best of my knowledge, I've never had an angel appear to me. I would hope, however, if this type of miracle ever occurred, the last thing I'd do is doubt *anything* an angel had to say. To question the Lord's messenger, to doubt, argue, or test the Lord in any way seems outlandish, and well… dumb! However, history tells us Zacharias wasn't the first to question the Lord or put Him to the test. He was just the latest.

Let's talk about Gideon, one of the Judges of Israel. If Zacharias was dumb, Gideon was dumber. When the Lord Himself spoke to Gideon, this young man not only questioned God; he had the temerity to test Him. Let's look at Judges 6:36-40.

*[36]Gideon said to God, "If you will save Israel by my hand as you have promised—[37]look, I will place a wool fleece on the threshing floor. If there is dew only on the fleece and all the ground is dry, then I will know that you will save Israel by my hand, as you said." [38]And that is what happened. Gideon rose early the next day; he squeezed the fleece and wrung out the dew—a bowlful of water. [39]Then Gideon said to God, "Do not be angry with me. Let me make just one more request. Allow me one more test with the fleece. This time, make the fleece dry and the ground covered with dew." [40]That night God did so. Only the fleece was dry; all the ground was covered with dew.*

The good Lord must have been in a great mood on that day in history because Gideon got away with his impertinence…twice! Poor unfortunate Zacharias, who came along much later, was punished for doing half as much. Yet, not only did Gideon get away with testing the Lord, he was subsequently used in a mighty way to bring glory to God's name.

Have you ever tested God, questioned His motives, or wondered if He knew what He was doing? Sure you have. I have, too. Though I've never had an angel appear to me with pronouncements about my future or the destiny of my people, still I have to admit, I've been dumb enough to question God. "Are you sure you want *me* to go?" "Do I really have to trust you *completely*?" "Wouldn't it be better if..."

I wish I were more like Mary, the mother of Jesus. When an angel appeared to her and changed her life in an instant, all she had to say in return was,

> [38] *"May it be to me as you have said*
> *—Luke 1:38."*

Who would you rather be—dumb, dumber or Mary? Yeah, I said Mary, too.

## PRAYING TOGETHER

*Father, how grateful I am, you are so
patient. So many times I've questioned you and
doubted you, put you to the test and still...you love
me. Still you gave your Son for me. I am so blessed
in your generosity. I thank you, God. Even when I'm
impertinent and "dumb," you use me to bring glory
to your name. I worship you and praise you,
Father! In the name of Christ Jesus, I pray—amen.*

## JOURNALING YOUR THOUGHTS

Though it may not be entirely intelligent,
questioning God seems to be a very human thing to
do. Take some time writing in your journal today
about a time when you might have questioned the
Lord Almighty. What happened?

Write about a time when you questioned
God.

Why did you have questions?

Is it hard for you to be like Mary?  If so,
why?

# Ruth

Falling between the books of Judges and 1 Samuel, in which warfare, murder and mayhem feature, the book of Ruth is a refreshing interlude. It is the story of the romance between Ruth, a young, widowed, Moabite woman and Boaz a Jewish land owner, the son of a prostitute. From their family line came the king of the Hebrew nation (David) and the King of Heaven, Jesus. The message is clear: God can use anyone—*no matter their background*—to further His kingdom.

# Some Enchanted Evening

*[4] Just then Boaz arrived from Bethlehem and greeted the harvesters, "The LORD be with you!" "The LORD blesses you," they answered. [5] Boaz asked the overseer of his harvesters, "Who does that young woman belong to?" —Ruth 2:4*

Peas in a pod, that's what my friend Kelly and I were. We were so much alike; we were often mistaken for sisters. We felt like sisters. We'd known each other our entire lives—our mothers had been sorority sisters. So, it was no surprise to anyone when, as little girls, we had all the same toys, played all the same games and watched all the same TV shows. As we grew, we ran in the same circles, belonged to the same clubs and dreamed of the same future career. We even dressed the same and wore our hair and make-up identically. We could not have been more…well, the same.

When it came to boys, however, we couldn't have been more different.

Kelly and I were barely sixteen when she began dating Tom. She liked to date big and burly guys with a little bit of "bad boy" in them. Tom was all that and more. He stood 6'6", weighed just over 300 pounds, and wore his hair long with a thick beard. What's more, Tom rode a motorcycle, had tattoos and listened to ZZ Top. Although he didn't belong to any motorcycle gangs, he sure looked like he did.

When Kelly started dating Tom I was between boyfriends. She tried to convince me to go out on a blind date with his roommate. I refused, emphatically. As sweet as Tom turned out to be, he scared me to death. I didn't want to imagine how frightening his roommate might be.

One day, she called and said, "We're on our way over. Brush your hair and take off that hideous shirt you wore to school today. Put on the pretty blue one." Then she hung up. Who did she mean when she said, "we"? Oh no, not the blind date! I dialed her right back but, she didn't answer. I was frantic. She wouldn't dare!

But, she did.

He was everything I had expected him to be—for the most part—a rocker with long dark hair, wearing ratty jeans and a faded rock band T-shirt. Although he didn't seem to have any tattoos, and wasn't quite as big as Tom, he wasn't exactly my cup of tea, either. However, I must admit, I couldn't help but notice his beautiful green eyes and nice shy smile.

"Well," I said, "I guess one date won't hurt anything." He shrugged and away we went.

Less than a year after that first date, the roommate (Lester) and I were married. Thirty-two years later, I still look into those same green eyes, every night before I go to sleep and thank God—*and Kelly*—for the man I love.

Love happened that fast for Ruth and Boaz too.

When we first meet Ruth, she is a young destitute widow living off the kindness of strangers, a Moabite in the land of Israel; her only friend her dead husband's mother. As her story develops, she finds herself in a field belonging to Boaz, a distant relative of her father-in-law's family. From the moment Boaz sees her gleaning in the field, he is taken with her; so much so he offers her—*and her mother-in-law*—his protection and care. They fall madly in love and in the end we see Ruth and Boaz married and parents to Obed, grandfather to King David.

There is a reason their story is included in the Bible. It is a wonderful illustration of how we come to faith in Christ. Like Ruth, we are first alone, living off of the dregs of the secular world, desperate and unsure. Then, from across eternity we see him—*Jesus*. From the moment our eyes meet, our fate is sealed. Just as Ruth could not resist Boaz, just as I could not resist Lester, neither can we resist the allure of Jesus' call; nor can we ignore His message. We fall completely in love with our Savior and in his arms we are made whole and pure.

Jesus looks beyond our inglorious past and sees who and what we can be in Him. He sees a future for us we could never imagine for ourselves. Think of Ruth who never would have envisioned herself as the great-grandmother of a king. As the son of a prostitute, Boaz could never have anticipated he'd be the ancestor to the Messiah. Yet, with God, something amazing came of their lives.

The same could be said of yours. Open yourself to His will, His plan. Allow Him to work in your life and He will prosper you further than your wildest dreams could ever take you. Yield yourself to Him and some enchanted evening…or morning… or noon… God will change your life and make it spectacular!

### PRAYING TOGETHER

*Oh God, how inspiring this story of Ruth and Boaz is to me, Jesus. I pray you can use me—I know you can use me—to bring glory to your name just as you did with them. Father, here I am. Send me. In the name of Jesus, our returning Savior, Amen.*

### JOURNALING YOUR THOUGHTS

A friend of mine once asked the following question, "How could God ever use *me*?" Are you kidding?  Rahab, the mother of Boaz, was a prostitute who helped bring down the walls of Jericho. Matthew was a tax collector. Paul began his story as a bigot and murderer of Christians. Yet, God used them all to bring glory to His name. He can use you too!

I do (or don't) believe that God can use me. Explain your answer.

(If) I do believe that God can use me, the question is: Am I willing?

How far will I go?  Explain

# 1 Samuel

The book of 1 Samuel tells the story of King David
and his predecessor to the throne, King Saul. It tells
how each man came to power and of the victories
*and failures* they experienced along the way.

# Put the Blame on Me

*²³When Abigail saw David, she quickly got off her
donkey and bowed down before David with her face
to the ground. ²⁴She fell at his feet and said: "My
lord, let the blame be on me alone. Hear what your
servant has to say."*
—*1 Samuel 25: 23-24*

Every few years, my husband and I travel
home to Texas to visit with friends and family. Each
time we do my mother says, "Are you sure there
isn't something you'd rather be doing than sitting
around talking to us?" She thinks that because we're
on "vacation" we should be off doing something
*exciting.*

I wish she'd believe me when I say I don't go to Texas to be a tourist. I grew up there. There isn't much I haven't already seen in the Lone Star State. When we go to Texas, we want to sit at my mother's dining room table and listen to our loved ones tell us what's new in their lives; we want to hear about their current girlfriends or boyfriends (or in some cases, spouses); we want to hear about jobs and kids and hobbies.

I, personally, love to listen to my mother talk about the friends we share. I want to hear the local chitchat and news, and I want to listen to my dad tell corny jokes. I can't wait, each visit, to hear my sister tell stories about her life. She's an incredible story-teller who can make me laugh and cry, get angry and be excited all within the same tale.

The best stories though, come from my brother. Every time we're together he tells the same three stories and each time he tells them, they grow larger and more fantastical. His favorite is about a blue glass chicken my mother once treasured. I say "once" because that chicken is long gone. One of the three of us broke it when we were children.

Although my brother took the blame, at the time—
and (according to him) the punishment—he's
always maintained he was not the guilty party and
swears, to this day, *I* am to blame for the chicken's
demise. I don't even remember the silly thing!
However, for many years now I've taken culpability
for the incident because…well, it's just easier and
makes his telling of the story funnier.

In our passage today we see someone else
taking the blame for something she didn't do. When
Abigail, the wife of Nabal, discovered her husband
had foolishly been disrespectful to the anointed
King David, she went into crisis mode by taking all
the blame on herself.

Let me tell you what happened.

While traveling through Nabal's territory,
David sent servants to Nabal to ask for food, water
and supplies for his men and himself. Nabal refused
by saying,

*[10"] Who is this David? Who is this son of Jesse?
Many servants are breaking away from their
masters these days. [11] Why should I take my bread
and water, and the meat I have slaughtered for my*

*shearers, and give it to men coming from who*
*knows where?" —1 Samuel 25: 10-11.*

When David heard of Nabal's response to
his request, he armed four hundred of his men and
went in search of the wealthy land owner. However,
when a servant told Abigail (Nabal's wife) about
David's request and her husband's reaction, she
knew she had to do something—and fast—to keep
her whole family from David's wrath.

She loaded grain, raisins and fig cakes,
along with slaughtered sheep, onto donkeys and
rode out to meet David before the worst could
happen. As she approached the king, she dropped
from her donkey and fell on her face before him,
and took the blame for her husband's insults and
surly nature.

Thanks to Abigail's quick thinking and
humble attitude, war was averted. David sent her on
her way, with thanks and gratitude and then he
feasted. When Abigail later told her husband what
had happened, the Bible says,

*37" ...his heart failed him and he became like a stone. 38About ten days later, the LORD struck Nabal and he died." —1 Samuel 25: 37-38.*

David was so impressed with Abigail that later, after Nabal's death, he married her.

Like Abigail, Jesus once took the blame for everything you and I have ever done to shame our King, his Father. Despite our ugly and sordid past, we were forgiven and brought into the throne room as adopted children of God. How blessed we are that Jesus was willing to take our blame. How grateful we should be that God is willing to forgive. All He asks in return is that we love Him. Hallelujah!

### *PRAYING TOGETHER*

*Oh Heavenly Father, how amazed I am by your loving heart! I praise you and worship you for being such a loving and caring Father that you would send your Son to take my blame. How grateful I am for His sacrifice—how shamed I am He had to make it. I can never repay His loving act. However, I will love you forever in return. I pray in*

*the name of the One True God, His Son and His*
*Spirit. Amen.*

### *JOURNALING YOUR THOUGHTS*

In 1973 the singing group Tony Orlando and Dawn, hit it big with the release of "Tie a Yellow Ribbon Round the Ole Oak Tree." The song tells the story of a just-released felon coming home from prison. The story-teller sings, "...*If I don't see a ribbon 'round the old oak tree, I'll stay on the bus, forget about us, put the blame on me, if I don't see a yellow ribbon 'round the old oak tree.*" Forgiven completely by his lady love, the man comes home to find hundreds of yellow ribbons attached to that old oak tree. As in the song, God forgives us everything if only we ask. Spend some time today journaling about the answers to those questions in the space below.

Do I need to forgive someone? Why haven't I?

Has my inability to forgive kept me from relating fully to God?

# 2 Samuel

Forming a more complete picture of God as a stern but loving and forgiving Father, the book of 2 Samuel covers a forty year period during David's reign over all of Israel; it is the summary of his later years as king. His triumphs and tragedies as a ruler—*and as a man*—serve as both a warning against sinful arrogance and as an example of humble servant hood.

# She Can't Be All Bad

*23 "Saul and Jonathan— in life they were loved and gracious, and in death they were not parted. They were swifter than eagles, they were stronger than lions." —2 Samuel 1:23*

Hate is a pretty strong emotion and one that Christians try to avoid as much as possible. However, I will admit there was a time, early in my Christian life, when I *hated* a fellow sister in Christ. I hated her…and it was killing me.

For as long as I'd known her, every time we were together, Lanie had gone out of her way to hurt my feelings and injure my pride. For fun! Or, so it seemed.

Once, at an Easter event, as I was reaching above my head to recapture a fly-away balloon, Lanie said, "Oh Angie, *honey*, be careful. Even dresses made for *big girls like you*, can only take so much tension before their seams just 'pop'." There were also cracks about my complexion ("What a shame make-up won't cover those big ugly blotches"), my hair ("You poor thing, I just don't know how you deal with such thin straggly hair") and my kids ("They're so cute in their little faded hand-me-down-outfits").

Her cut-to-the-bone but oh-so-sweetly delivered jabs were humiliating and incredibly painful. After one particularly hurtful jab, I ran to the ladies' room in angry tears. Thinking I was alone, I hissed through my teeth to the mirror on the wall— *"I hate that woman."* Only…I wasn't alone. A toilet flushed in a far stall and out stepped Martha, the associate pastor's wife. I wanted to die of embarrassment! Martha was smiling as she walked up to the sink and began to wash her hands. Our eyes met in the mirror and she whispered, "Lanie rubs me the wrong way, too."

Martha had seen (on more than one occasion) how Lanie treated me and empathized. She and I had a long talk that day during which she told me I had every right to respond to Lanie's taunts and insults with anger and frustration. However, she explained, to do so would not only hurt Jesus but give the enemy a treat. "Satan loves it when Christians fight amongst themselves. It's like chocolate syrup on his steaming bowl of hot hate."

Martha made two suggestions: "First," she said, "Try finding something about Lanie you can like or can relate to. For instance, her children adore her. She must be a pretty good mom. You're a mom, too, and a good one. Try relating to how stressful her life must be—she runs two businesses, a home and a marriage. She's rarely *at* home. Still, she has two great kids who think she's wonderful. She can't be all bad." Second, Martha recommended I try using graciousness to combat Lanie's insults. "The next time she tells you your kids look great in hand-me-downs…thank her for the compliment. Don't *re*act in anger, act with deliberate graciousness, instead."

Graciousness, Martha told me, can be a healing balm for everyone.

Israel's King David must have been given this very same advice.

Our scripture today comes from the eulogy delivered by King David at the funeral of Jonathan and his father, David's predecessor, King Saul. They died in battle fighting side-by-side. David honored them both with these lovely words:

*"Saul and Jonathan—in life they were loved and gracious, and in death they were not parted. They were swifter than eagles, they were stronger than lions." —2 Samuel 1:23*

Jonathan was David's best friend and soul-mate. It's easy to imagine David saying such charming words about him. Yet, to say those same words about Saul, who hated David, who tried to kill him on more than one occasion, who ran him out of town, making him an out-law; Saul ruined his marriage *and more…* Well, it seems rather hypocritical. Doesn't it?

No.

You see, David remembered Saul was not all bad. In fact, at the beginning of their relationship, David had loved and admired Saul very much and the feeling was mutual. Although it took Saul's tragic death for David to recover those memories, he was eventually able to put aside his hurt and anger and remember the good in Saul.

When you find yourself on the edge of hating someone, perhaps you can try instead to realize she (or he) can't be all bad. Search for her redeeming qualities. We all have them. As long as she's not out kicking puppies or clubbing baby seals, there's got to be something about her you can relate to in a good way. And before you ask yourself *"What Would Jesus Do"*, know the answer is already within your heart. Love her anyway. **Love. Her. Anyway.** She can't be all bad.

### *PRAYING TOGETHER*

*Father, we pray you can plant in our hearts a love for one another, stronger than any petty jealousy, dislike, or dishonesty; teach us to find the good in each other, to search out those things which make each of us special. We don't have to be the best of friends, Father, but we do need to love one another as you commanded us to do. I pray in the name of Jesus. Amen.*

### *JOURNALING YOUR THOUGHTS*

Just as germs make our bodies sick, anger and hate injure our souls. Today, I'd like to encourage you to spend a little time thinking about what might be making you heartsick. Use the questions below as a 'jumping off point' to your journaling.

If I were being honest with myself *and God,* I might admit that I hate_____. Explain why.

What might I do to change the way I feel about this person?

# 1 Kings

The book of 1 Kings begins with the death of King David and follows the reign of his son and successor, Solomon. Along the way, God shares several stories of great importance…this is one.

---

# Don't Believe Everything You Hear

*[18]The old prophet answered, "I too am a prophet, as you are. And an angel said to me by the word of the LORD: 'Bring him back with you to your house so that he may eat bread and drink water.' "(But he was lying to him.) [19]So the man of God returned with him and ate and drank in his house.*

*—1 Kings 13: 18-19*

The phone rang. I answered it and was greeted very strangely. "You're never going to believe this!" I responded, "Um…hello?"

"Oh, hi, it's Kathy. I'm calling on behalf of the prayer circle. I have a prayer request and you're never going to believe it." As Kathy filled me in on what we were supposed to be praying about, I realized she was right—I didn't believe it!

Our mutual friend and fellow church member, Dana, had just activated the prayer circle with an emergency prayer request. The concern, according to Kathy, was Dana's pregnancy; it was suddenly at risk. She was in danger of losing her baby. The doctor had prescribed bed rest and prayer. That's where we came in.

"Dana's pregnant?!" I squealed into the phone, "When did this happen? She's forty-four years old! Why didn't she tell me she was having a baby?" Dana and I were very close, or so I thought. Yet, *obviously*, I'd been completely left out of the loop!

My husband walked into the kitchen just as I hung up the phone. I filled him in on the news I'd just received. "You better call Dana," he said. He was right. I should have called Dana before taking another breath. But, I was trained as a member of the prayer circle to keep the phone lines buzzing until the prayer had gone all the way through the circle and everyone had prayed. So, I called the next person on the phone list and passed the concern on to her just as I had received it. *"You're not going to believe this..."*

Later, when I could stand it no longer, I called Dana and bombarded her with questions. The last one I asked was, "Is there anything I can do?" "Yes, there is," she replied, "You can answer a question: Why are you telling people I'm pregnant?" My stomach sank... uh oh.

As it turns out, Dana had activated the prayer circle for her co-worker and friend, **Deanna.** I suddenly felt very stupid—especially after Dana reminded me I had visited her in the hospital just a few months before *when she had her hysterectomy.* I let her have her grins and giggles at my expense and then quickly hung up to begin the "clean up" calls.

The next Sunday our Pastor delivered a very timely sermon entitled, "Don't Believe Everything You Hear".

He spoke on 1 Kings, chapter 13, which is devoted to just one story. It's a tale about a prophet—a man of God—whom the Lord sent to deliver a message to the wicked king of Judah. God instructed the prophet to deliver his message and then get out of Dodge.

*⁹"You must not eat bread or drink water or return by the way you came". —1 Kings 13:9*

On his way out of town the prophet stopped to rest beneath a tree. Another man came along claiming to also be a man of God. He said he'd been sent by the Lord to bring the first man back to his home for food, drink and rest. Sadly, the second man lied.

As the story goes, God becomes so angry with his prophet—for so blatantly disobeying his orders *not* to eat, *not* to drink and *not* to go back the way he had come—He allowed him (the prophet) to be killed by a lion as punishment.

As often happens with Bible stories we're left with many questions. Why did God prohibit the first man from eating, drinking and resting? Why did the second man lie? Who sent him and for what purpose?

We may never know.

What we do know is this—we should never believe everything we hear, even if it's coming from another child of God.

Some of the worst lies (gossip, slander, bigotry and misinformation) are told under the banner of Christian camaraderie. Some of the vilest gossip sessions begin with the words, *"we need to pray for..."*

The thing we must always remember is: just because a story makes the rounds under the umbrella of a prayer request or Christian concern, that doesn't mean it's true, accurate or worthy of repetition. Don't believe everything you hear. Trust only in the Holy Spirit and God's Word.

How will you know when information you're given is untrue or unwise? Listen to the Holy Spirit within you. He will knock loudly upon your heart when he hears an untruth, or the beginnings of a piece of gossip or slander. If you will listen—*only to Him*—he'll lead you in the right way to go.

### PRAYING TOGETHER

*Father in heaven, how grateful I am for your Holy Spirit living within me. I ask that you would*

*open my heart and eyes and ears to His guiding.*
*Show me the way to pay attention when He speaks.*
*He isn't just a passenger in my soul—He is an*
*active, loving, caring participant in my life who*
*wants to help me. I pray these things in the name of*
*your Son, the mighty counselor. Amen.*

### JOURNALING YOUR THOUGHTS

Use this time to gauge your connection with the Holy Spirit who lives within you. Ask yourself two, three or all of the following questions to determine if you and the Helper need help.

Do I share information that isn't mine to share? Do I listen when the Spirit tries to stop me?

Do I need to make changes in the way I relate to God's Holy Spirit within me and others around me? If so, what steps do I need to take?

# 2 Kings

Covering a period of 250 years, the book of 2 Kings tells the stories of all the different rulers—good and bad—who led the Hebrew nation after the deaths of kings David and Solomon. Two major happenings are recorded in this book. First, because of the sins of the people the Lord allowed the Assyrians to destroy the Northern Kingdom of Israel in or around the year 772 B.C. (detailed in chapter 17) and second, the Babylonians were allowed to do the same to the Southern Kingdom in 586 B.C. (chapters 24 & 25). However, throughout this time in history God continued to work for His people, mainly through miracles, messages and signs delivered by the prophet Elisha.

# Good to the Last Drop

*[3] Elisha said, "Go around and ask all your neighbors for empty jars. Don't ask for just a few. [4] Then go inside and shut the door behind you and your sons. Pour oil into all the jars, and as each is filled, put it to one side." [5] She left him and*

*afterward shut the door behind her and her sons.*
*They brought the jars to her and she kept pouring.*
*[6]When all the jars were full, she said to her son,*
*"Bring me another one." But he replied, "There is*
*not a jar left." Then the oil stopped flowing. [7]She*
*went and told the man of God, and he said, "Go,*
*sell the oil and pay your debts. You and your sons*
*can live on what is left." —2 Kings 4:3-7*

Did you know President Theodore Roosevelt is credited with giving the Maxwell House brand of coffee their slogan, the one they would use for more than one hundred years? As the story goes, good old Teddy had a coffee habit as big as his personality. While touring Hermitage House (the estate of seventh president Andrew Jackson), Roosevelt asked for and was served a cup of (Maxwell House) coffee. After his last sip he declared it to be "good to the last drop". [1]

I thought of that particular advertising slogan—*good to the last drop*—as I studied our scripture reading for today. Let me tell you why.

The woman in our study passage was a resident of the Northern Kingdom of Israel—long

before the Assyrians destroyed it. The whole
country was in a huge mess. King Jehoram had
turned his back on God and led his people to do the
same, establishing the deification of a golden calf.
He also encouraged the continued worship of the
pagan god, Baal, a practice his mother, Jezebel, had
begun. Angry and hurt because of their idolatry,
God withdrew his blessings from Israel.

Happily, however, not everyone in the
nation had turned from the worship of the one true
God. Many still believed in the great "I AM." As a
matter of fact, in some places, certain men and their
whole families gathered to study and meditate on
God's Word. These communities of religious men
were often called "the sons of prophets". The
honorary heads of these religious Bible schools
were often the leading prophets of the day; Elisha
was such a man.

The woman in our scripture reference for
today was the widow of one of these religious
students. When Elisha visited the worshiping
community, she claimed his attention and reminded
him of whom her husband had been. Then, with
humility she pointed out how devoted her husband

had been to the Lord *and to Elisha.* She was not after Elisha's pity—she wanted his help!

She had been left destitute by her husband's death, and his creditors were banging on the door threatening to take her children, as slaves, to pay the debt. Luckily, Elisha *did* remember her husband and in his honor wanted to do what he could to help her family.

He said, "Tell me, what do you have in your house?" The woman explained the only thing she had left in the world was a little bit of oil in a very small jar (a prized commodity in those days). Elisha told the woman to gather as many pots and urns as she could. Then, he instructed her to fill those pots with the oil she had left in her own small jar. She must have thought he was crazy. Hadn't she already told him she had only a little oil left? However, she did as he asked.

Imagine her surprise when the oil poured and poured *and poured* only giving out when she ran out of pots to put it in! She was able to sell the pots filled with olive oil and made enough money to pay off her creditors, save her children from slavery and live comfortably for the rest of her life. How good is our God?

For some of us, crisis is a way of life, but it's no way to live!

When you find yourself in dire straits like the widow, call out to the Lord! Remind Him of His promises. Then, go out and get yourself some pots, girl! The Good Lord will fill your heart to the brim with love of Him.

### PRAYING TOGETHER

*Yahweh Yireh, God who provides, I worship you for being so incredibly generous and loving. From Your heart pours forth such a surplus of love and care. Though I may exist in a state of crisis, I do not live there. Thank you, Lord. I trust in you. Amen.*

### JOURNALING YOUR THOUGHTS

How amazingly generous is our God! He will not leave you weak and weary. He will fill you to the brim with blessings—if only you ask. Write in your journal today about a time (or many times) when God filled you spiritually to overflowing.

Write about a time when you were empty spiritually.

Did you call out to the Lord to fill you up again? If so, what happened?

There are times when every Christian uses the last of his/her reserves. When this happens to you, what steps do you take to fill them up again?

Online Resources:

[1] Theodore Roosevelt Association, Rogena L. Jeffries site editor, *Theodore Roosevelt Association, The Life of Theodore Roosevelt Myths, Legends & Trivia,* http://www.theodoreroosevelt.org/life/Maxwell.htm

# 1 Chronicles

Written from the viewpoint of priests, 1 & 2 Chronicles are parallel versions of the same stories we found in 1 & 2 Samuel and 1 & 2 Kings. This book begins with a detailed genealogical history of King David's line. With a special prominence given to the religious affairs of state, the story that follows begins with David's ascension as king of Israel (as in 1 Kings) and ends with Solomon's succession to his father's throne.

# Marking My Territory

*[10]Jabez cried out to the God of Israel, "Oh that you would bless me and enlarge my territory! Let your hand be with me, and keep me from harm so that I will be free from pain." And God granted his request. —1 Chronicles 4:10*

Dr. Bruce Wilkinson is a dynamic and inspirational speaker and the author of over sixty books including *Walk Through the Bible* and *You Were Born for This.* One of his most recent works,

*The Prayer of Jabez,* was once called the fastest selling book of all time (beliefnet.com). According to the New York Times Best Seller List, this popular inspirational work has sold more than nine million copies world wide since its publication date in 2000.

That name—Jabez—is buried in the lists of "begats" most of us only skim (or skip altogether) when reading our Bibles. You know the ones I mean, *"...Shem begat Arphaxad whom begat Salah whom begat Eber whom begat...."* I've never gotten through the fifth chapter of Genesis (where many of the Biblical family lines are detailed) without falling asleep. I bet like me, many of Bruce Wilkinson's 9 million readers had no idea Jabez even existed before reading his book. However, I would also be willing to bet their lives were changed, as mine was, by this fascinating story.

Jabez is mentioned just once, in 1 Chronicles 4:9-10, which reads:

*[9] Jabez was more honorable than his brothers. His mother had named him Jabez, saying," I gave birth to him in pain." [10] Jabez cried out to the God of*

*Israel, "Oh that you would bless me and enlarge my territory! Let your hand be with me, and keep me from harm so that I will be free from pain." And God granted his request.*

After reading Wilkinson's book I was moved to pray this same prayer. I'm not sure what I was hoping for; I knew I wanted to be a writer, a speaker, and Biblical teacher. I knew I wanted to change hearts and lives. I was also keenly aware of wanting to be free of all harm and pain; and—I'll admit it–I wanted to be rich and famous. Who doesn't?

Of course, I was disappointed. Nothing exciting happened to me or *in* me even though I prayed that prayer every night for several months. I remember complaining to a friend about the lack of expansion in my life. I said, "God isn't working in me the way I had expected Him to. I've been praying the prayer of Jabez and nothing has happened."

She replied, "How do you know that? How do you know God hasn't done exactly what you asked Him to do?"

"Because," I said, "I'm still dirt poor, unpublished and unknown. How can I expand my territory if I'm a nobody?"

My friend, a very sophisticated, genteel and refined older woman, popped me on the forehead with the heel of her palm. In the depths of my shock I heard her say, "You're not a nobody you're an idiot."

God, she explained, was not a bank from which I could withdraw a better life just because I wanted it. God, she said, would use me (not the other way around) to bring glory to His kingdom when, where and how *He* saw fit. She went on to say that in her opinion my prayers *had* been answered. I was just too dumb to see it.

"You have brought the Word of God and changed the lives of at least two people just in the last year. Those two people are now children of the Lord. How do you know they aren't a part of your *'territory'*?" She went on, "You reached out to them. They'll reach out to others. Each one will reach one and so on and so on. Voilà! Expanded territory!" She grinned. "Your trouble is you're defining the word territory to be something more materialistic than it might be in God's plan."

She was right, of course. I was so concerned with my own ideals of what my territory should be I never once thought to consider what it really was and to *whom* it really belonged to in the first place.

We have to be very careful not to allow ourselves to dream of what *we* want, where *we* want to go, and how *we* want to get there. We have to dream in terms of what's best for *His* kingdom, not ours. We have to be willing to do what He wants us to do and to go where He wants us to go. Once we do that, God will provide the way and the wherewithal. I often have to remind myself God answers every prayer. I just have to listen for the answer He's willing to give, and not the one I want to hear. Ask yourself if you need to do the same.

### *PRAYING TOGETHER*

*Father, I pray you will forgive my ego and my insane desire to store up for myself riches on earth when I know my treasure in heaven is worth so much more. I pray you will use me instead to expand your kingdom however, whenever and*

*wherever you see fit. Mold me and make me into*
*your will. Here am I Father, waiting and still!*
*Amen.*

## *JOURNALING YOUR THOUGHTS*

Have you ever been disappointed by
unanswered prayer? Did it really go unanswered or
did you miss the reply because it wasn't what you
wanted to hear? Find a quiet corner to curl up in,
with your journal, and spend some time recording
your thoughts about what you want out of life
versus what God wants for you instead.

I have been disappointed in the past by
what I thought was an unanswered prayer. Give an
example:

In hindsight I can see that God gave
me instead, _____. Tell the story.

I have recently asked God
for_____. Am I listening for the answer
He's willing to give or the one I want to hear?

# 2 Chronicles

2 Chronicles continues the history of Judah, the southern portion of Israel, while putting major emphasis on the occasional spiritual (re)awakenings during the region's decline. This book could be seen as the "Pollyanna" of the Bible; for the most part, mostly positive stories abound. Very little is mentioned, in 2 Chronicles, of the bad kings—*and there were bad kings*—or the negative consequences of their actions. However, it is from this positive spin we can see a foreshadowing of the King of kings, Jesus Christ.

# Bible Black Belt

*[14]If my people, who are called by my name, will humble themselves and pray and seek my face and turn from their wicked ways, then will I hear from heaven and will forgive their sin and will heal their land. —2 Chronicles 7:14*

My friend, Leslie, is an amazingly busy girl. She works full time as a kindergarten teacher at a local private Christian school, has four children who range in age from four to seventeen and has a part-time job as a judo instructor (she has a 6th degree Black Belt in Judo). Her loving husband, Ken, is a big help. However, he travels quite a bit for his job. This means Leslie is often left on her own to manage the kids, two large dogs, six bunnies, two lizards, and one ferret—not to mention two turtles.

Leslie and I were both members of the Women's Mentoring Ministry at our church and for a season, I was her mentor. One day while at lunch together, we were discussing how hectic our lives had become. She said, "I barely have time to breathe some days, but I always make time for personal Bible study. I have it all worked out. I get up at five and shower, dress and make my coffee. While the coffee is brewing, I blow-dry my hair and put on make-up. Then, with a fresh cup of java nearby to keep my concentration high, I read the Bible, a few pages of my PEOPLE magazine and the newspaper. Then, I pray. By 6:00 a.m., I'm on my way to work. It's a tight schedule, but I make sure to follow it everyday."

"Wow, that's great." I said. "But, let me ask; how much *quality* time do you really think you spend praying and studying?"

"What do you mean by 'quality time'," she asked.

I invited her to really think about her morning routine. "It seems kind of rushed to me, from the outside looking in. Do you spend much time *truly* soaking up His Spirit, listening to His voice? Or, to quote a catch phrase, are you just phoning it in?"

I told her about a sermon I'd heard as a child. The preacher had brought a toy telephone with him as a visual aid. He pretended to call God on the phone. Very quickly he summarized his wants and needs and told God exactly how he thought they should each be handled. Then, he explained to the Lord, during his imaginary conversation, just how busy he was. He dropped an obligatory "nice talking to you, God" and hung up. The preacher then asked those of us in the congregation, "Is this the way your talks with God go? Do you give the Lord time to respond; to tell you *His* wants and wishes for your life? Do you take time to truly hear His voice deep in your heart? Or, are you just too busy to engage in an actual two-way conversation?"

I heard this sermon when I was eleven years old. I still remember it to this day.

Don't get me wrong. I told Leslie and I'll tell you, my relationship with God is just like yours—imperfect and sometimes sloppy (on my side of it anyway). I'm no expert on "quality time" or any other aspect of spirituality. However, as Leslie's mentor, I felt God prodding me to bring her this message. Now, I feel Him prodding me to bring it to you. God wants to be more to us than just another chore we feel obligated to slide into our busy schedules.

It isn't important whether you spend five minutes, thirty minutes or two hours each day with God. There are dozens of programs out there that teach you how to spend quality time with Him in just five minutes a day. What *is* important is how you spend your time with him. Make it count. Don't slip Him in between Brittany Spears and the local weather. During your time together put Him first in your heart and mind.

Remember, we always have time for the things we put first.

### PRAYING TOGETHER

*Father in heaven, how wonderful it is to take time each day with you to listen to your heartbeat and to hear your Words. I pray, Father, all of your daughters will humble themselves and seek your face each and every day, for quality time that matters; especially me. I pray in the name of your precious son, Jesus. Amen.*

### JOURNALING YOUR THOUGHTS

Take this chance to evaluate your study and prayer time. Do you need to make changes? If so, pray and ask God to help you find the will and the way to schedule time into your every day (no matter how much or how little) for quality time with Him and His Word. Then, follow through. It's just that simple.

Journal the thoughts, feelings, ideas and messages you may receive from God on this matter.

# Ezra

For seventy long years the people of Israel were held captive in the land of Babylon. The book of Ezra tells the story of their return to a homeland scarred and beaten. Solomon's glorious temple lay in ruin. Once home, God stirred the hearts of the people to rebuild their Temple and heal their land. Along with Zerubbabel and Nehemiah, Ezra led the people to accomplish their goals and triumph over old miseries and new trials.

# Generation Gap

*¹²Old men who had seen the first temple wept with a loud voice.* —Ezra 3:12 *(ESV)*

Each Sunday the choir at my church starts the service by leading the congregation in the most amazing contemporary praise music. It gets my heart pumping and wakes my spirit right up. I wouldn't miss that time of worship for anything in the world! I don't want to be even one second late.

My friend, Emma, feels differently, however. Emma deliberately arrives twenty minutes late to church every week because she has no desire to hear what she calls *"the hippy praise music."* She prefers slower, statelier hymns and more traditional instrumental music to the modern upbeat worship tunes heard in many church services today. Knowing this about her, but not knowing Emma personally, you might think she's an elderly woman, an old fogey. She's not. She's barely thirty years old.

I'm the old fogey.

However, musical opinions are like noses. Everyone has one and each one is different.

Unfortunately, across America, many churches have split in two, or dissolved completely over this issue of worship styles. One side of the aisle wants hymns; the other wants praise music. One side wants to hear only the organ and the other side wants to hear the electric keyboard. One side wants to shout "hallelujah" and the other wants to sit quietly and be moved in a more personal and private manner. Sadly, this is not a new argument.

When the Temple of Solomon was rebuilt, scripture tells us while the younger generation rejoiced (Ezra 3:10-11), the older generation wept (v12). Why would there be such polar opposite reactions to such a glorious moment?

The rejoicing of the younger generation is quite understandable. They felt triumphantly connected to the spectacular new temple and took pride in having overcome so many trials and tribulations to build it. In their excitement and jubilation (just as some worshippers do today), they opened their palms and lifted their hands to the Lord. They danced. They played tambourines and beat drums. They laughed and cried. They unlocked their hearts and sang with joy and adulation to the God of their ancestors.

It sounds to me like they went a little wild. And, that's okay. It was a momentous occasion.

The reaction of the older generation was somewhat different. Although the new temple *was* glorious, it was not quite equal in grandeur to the original. The older generation wept for the lost splendor and magnificence of Solomon's first temple. They may have also been mourning the loss of their past, their youth, and the time when they felt led to worship so exuberantly. Even though they were thrilled to have the new temple, they did grieve for what was lost.

As a member of the "older" generation, I can relate. Although I love the new praise music, I sometimes miss the organ and the old standby hymns of my youth.

However, when it comes to worship I'm just as happy swinging my arms in the air and singing **D.C. Talk** songs as I am sitting quietly and humming *Amazing Grace*. For me, it's not *how* I worship that's important. What matters the most is my desire to worship God with **_all_** of me.

God doesn't care about our musical choices or our style of dress. He doesn't care whether we sit or stand, wave our hands in the air or sit with them folded in our laps. He doesn't care if we're young or old, men or women, fat or lean. All God wants from us…is *all* of us. God wants to feel our hearts reaching out to him in adoration! He wants to be the object of our affection. Without true heart and soul worship of Him, none of the rest matters anyway!

Whatever your style of worship may be, remember to keep God as the center of your world—in church services and out. Keep His Word and His Will as the focus of your heart and mind and you can't go wrong. The rest is just window dressing.

### PRAYING TOGETHER

*Glorious and Wonderful Maker, I can't help thinking of how marvelous it is that you created each of us to be unique. You created us to like different things and to want to worship you in different ways. I pray, Father, we will all learn to worship you fully and wholly as our only focus. New, old, less grand, more magnificent—it shouldn't matter as long as we are worshipping you! I pray in the name of your Son, Amen.*

### JOURNALING YOUR THOUGHTS

Today, I would ask you to think about your heart as it concerns your worship of God. Journal about where your thoughts and feelings may have been the last time you worshipped. Were they focused on him, or something else?

When you worshipped last (whether at church or privately at home or anywhere else) what was your heart focused on?

If you can honestly say anything other than God, write in your journal about what kept your attention away from Him and try to come up with a strategy to keep it from happening in the future.

Write a prayer asking God to help you focus your attention on him during worship.

# Nehemiah

As governor of Judah, Nehemiah had great
influence in the city of Jerusalem. He was charged
with rebuilding the walls of the city. He was,
however, met with great opposition by enemies of
the state who wished to keep the city (and the
nation) vulnerable. Those around Nehemiah wanted
to meet violence with violence. But Nehemiah
refused to give in to hatred. He prayed to God for
strength and perseverance and was rewarded with
the defeat of his enemies and a completed city wall.

# Enemy Mine

*[9]They were all trying to frighten us, thinking, "Their
hands will get too weak for the work, and it will not
be completed." But I prayed, "Now strengthen my
hands." —Nehemiah 6:9*

I knew Jenny and I weren't going to get
along her very first day on the job. There was just
something about her that rubbed me the wrong way.
Evidently, the feeling was mutual. She told a co-

worker *(who couldn't wait to tell me)* she thought I was "stuck-up." I countered by calling her a "bleached blonde dimwit." Not my finest moment.

By the end of Jenny's first week in my office, she and I had shared two spats. By the end of her first month, we rarely spoke to each other at all unless it was to be sarcastic or rude.

After several years of petty nonsense, Jenny took the whole thing to a new level when she involved our supervisor. We were both up for the same position, but I had more experience and seniority. In our union-operated office, there was really no way Jenny could outbid me for the job. Everyone was surprised she even tried.

She went to our supervisor and accused me of several things I had not done and implied I was unfit for the position. In retaliation, I went to the supervisor and tattled on her for things she *had* done. Although I eventually won the position and was promoted, it did not come without a struggle, a great deal of embarrassment <u>and</u> an employee review for both Jenny and me with our "big" boss.

During those separate interviews, he wanted to know why we didn't get along. Although our feud had been going for almost three years, neither of us really knew why. We were both told to end it or end our careers. This was not a period of my life I'm proud of or would talk about if I didn't have a point to make.

We all have people and things in our lives we could call *enemies*. For me, it was Jenny. For some, it might be an emotion like fear, anxiety or depression. For still others, the thing they battle against could be an addiction. Satan will use any tool he can and will find a way to worm into our lives if we allow it.

Nehemiah, the man quoted in our scripture passage today, also had enemies. However, when he was faced with ridicule and mocking from his rivals, he ignored it. When that tactic didn't work, his opponents began to slander and threaten him. That didn't work either. Eventually, they resorted to cheap tricks, violence and vandalism.

Those are also Satan's tactics. He has no right to use them on us because Jesus came to break the bonds of slavery. We don't need to be bound to our hatred, jealousies and petty feuds. We don't need to continue in fear and depression. We don't have to continue being tied to those addictions that ruin our lives. Remember what Paul said: [12]*"I will not be mastered by anything"* (1 Corinthians 6:12).

Just like Paul, we are under the Lord's protection. We are covered by His power. Nehemiah knew this, too. When he was threatened by the opposition, he prayed. He prayed to God for strength and resolve, and God answered him!

God will answer you, too! There's no need to be a slave to your anger, your addiction or even your version of Jenny. Ask God to strengthen your hand, your determination, and your willpower. Fight against the opposition using the best weapon at your disposal—God's love.

### PRAYING TOGETHER

*Gracious Father, thank you for helping me to face my enemies, without hate and anger but with Christian love, patience and kindness. Thank you for giving me the tools to grow in wisdom and recognize Satan's hand in my relationships. I cannot fight what I cannot see, but in your wisdom you have given me the ability to know when the prince of this world is working in my life. You've given me the weapons with which to fight THE ENEMY—devotion, endurance and compassion. He cannot win against me when you are on my side. I pray, in the name of Jesus. Amen.*

### *JOURNALING YOUR THOUGHTS*

The enemy is on the job. Each day he brings into our lives something or someone that will weaken us and ruin us *if we allow it*.

What weapon does the enemy use against you? (Is it a person, a substance, an emotion, etc.?)

How do you fight against it? Or do you?

Have you entrusted this situation to the Lord? If not, why not?

# Esther

This chronicle of Israelite history takes place in time while many Jews were still in captivity in Babylon. The heroine of the story, Esther, is one of these. Against her will she is placed into the harem of King Xerxes of Babylon. She eventually captured the king's affection and became his queen.

---

# Say "Yes" to Be Blessed

*[14]If you keep quiet at this time, someone else will help and save the Jewish people, but you and your father's family will all die. And who knows, you may have been chosen queen for just such a time as this." —Esther 4:14*

Nancy hadn't slept in weeks. She had developed dark shadows beneath her eyes and creases around her mouth from the almost-constant frown she'd been wearing. She just looked exhausted and worn down. Plus, the lack of rest was beginning to show in her attitude and her countenance. As a matter of fact, her personality had taken such a huge u-turn away from her normally sweet and kindly disposition, people were beginning to truly worry about her.

"I'm just so tired," Nancy said to a group of us one day at lunch.

"What's keeping you up?" someone asked.

"I think it may be God. I think He's trying to tell me something."

It was suggested maybe she should stop ignoring God and listen to what He might be trying to tell her. Maybe then she could get a peaceful night's rest.

Nancy recalled her sleeping troubles began right about the time a friend had asked her to become a part of the ladies' praise team at church. The position as the alto in the Praise Team quartet would require a great deal of practice, time and commitment. It was a popular group and Nancy *did* want to be a part of it. However, she just couldn't bring herself to say "yes." She was just so busy. Nancy asked for a few weeks to pray and think about the offer. Then she promptly put it aside and tried not think about it all.

In the weeks that followed our conversation, several things happened that left Nancy feeling a bit unsettled—*pleasantly* so. She had begun to pray God would answer the "should I or shouldn't I" question concerning the praise team. Suddenly, her schedule began to lighten. Her work load at the office began to even out. The client who had insisted on meeting twice weekly suddenly agreed to meet with Nancy just once a month. And, a co-worker offered to take another client case completely leaving Nancy with a little freer time. At home, her daughter made arrangements with a friend to carpool to school, and her son found his own way to and from his job at the mall. Even other church commitments reduced their schedule or ended.

Nancy told another friend she was thinking seriously about accepting the position on the praise team. "But," she said, "I really need a sign from God that this is what I'm supposed to do." Her friend replied, "Do you need a truck to fall on your head?" So Nancy accepted the position on the ladies' praise team and soon settled into an easy pattern of rehearsals, practices and performances. What a blessing she had been given by God!

After a few months on the praise team, Nancy was asked to sing a solo at the funeral of a dear friend's mother. Nancy chose to sing a song by Amy Grant entitled "I Will Remember You." After the service, the dear friend, Linda, pulled Nancy aside to tell her how much she appreciated her song. "I wanted to remember my mother as the happy, smiling, joyful person she was. Now, every time I hear that song I'll be able to remember this day with a smile." As Nancy related this story to a group of us a few days later, one person said, "Aren't you glad you stopped ignoring God when he was trying to lead you into ministry?"

God places each of us into positions where we can reach out and grab those chances to bring glory to His name. Some are given fortuitous opportunities to evangelize in big and small ways. Others are given rare chances to minister to those in need. Still more are given the chance to lead, as Nancy was.

However, if we ignore God's call, turn away and pretend we aren't ready or justify our negligence with excuses; if we choose to pass on our blessings, God *will* find someone else to do the job. He will bless someone else with opportunities to evangelize. He will find someone else to minister to those in need. He will find someone else to lead. Those who say "yes" will be blessed to overflowing while those who say "no" will be left empty and unsatisfied.

If Esther had said "no," many could have suffered for her fear and disobedience. Eventually, God would have raised another to take her place, but Esther would have lost the blessing God wanted to bestow on *her*.

In the same way, if Nancy had said "no" to God's opportunity, He would have found another to bless her dear friend Linda, but what would Nancy have lost? God challenges all of us to rise above where we are and meet Him where *He* is so He can bless us with untold miracles. Don't let fear and cowardice keep you from answering His call. The will of God will never take you to a place where the grace of God cannot protect and bless you. Say "yes" and be blessed!

## PRAYING TOGETHER

*Dear God, how wonderful you are! We are so grateful to be given the opportunity to serve in your kingdom. Give us all the strength to answer, "Here I am Lord. Send me." I pray in the name of Jesus who went when you called and gave all he had to give. Amen.*

## JOURNALING YOUR THOUGHTS

In movies, the president of the United States is often portrayed as getting and making very important calls on the "hotline" or red telephone. We all get those kinds of "hotline" calls from God. He calls to wake us up and let us know what to say, when to say it, where to be and what to do when we get there. The problem is we often ignore the phone when it rings.

When was the last time I received a "hotline" call from God?

Did I answer when He called?

# Job

Written in the form of didactic poetry (meant to both entertain and instruct) the book of Job deals with the age-old question:
Why is there suffering in the world when our God is powerful enough to end it?

# Oh Woe Is Me

*³ If only I knew where to find him; if only I could go to his dwelling! ⁴I would state my case before him and fill my mouth with arguments. ⁵I would find out what he would answer me, and consider what he would say to me. —Psalm 46: 3-5*

Evan was through with God. In one year he had lost his parents and wife to a drunk driver, and his sister to suicide. Understandably, he found himself mired in depression and he could not seem to break away from it. So, he quit his job, sold his home, and moved to the other side of the country in an attempt to escape his pain. It only followed him to California. The sunny beaches and beautiful people there only served to deepen his sadness and remind him of all he had lost.

On a walk one Saturday he ran into a coworker who was jogging with a friend. As the three men stood on the sidewalk talking, Evan's coworker said, "We're playing basketball tonight at our church. Want to join us?" Evan politely refused, thinking he'd never step foot in a church again— even by way of a pick-up game. "I hate God!" he thought.

A few weeks later, a stranger at the grocery store placed a Bible tract in Evan's hand that read, "Salvation Guaranteed or Your Sins Cheerfully Refunded." Evan couldn't suppress a smile, but quickly erased it when he remembered he was mad at God. On his way out of the store, he tossed the tract in a trashcan.

God wasn't willing to be tossed away so casually. He wasn't done with Evan yet.

Two days later, Evan was surprised to receive a phone call from his hometown pastor. After catching up with one another, the pastor said, "Can we pray together now?" Evan almost said no, but he didn't want to hurt the pastor's feelings, so he agreed. However, the moment the man began to pray, *"Heavenly Father…"* Evan cut him off, pretending there was a knock at his door and hung up quickly after a rather hurried goodbye.

For days afterwards, Evan was irritable and anxious. He paced around his office and apartment, feeling like a cat closed up in a bag. He was a nervous wreck. So, when his friend from work again invited him to play basketball, Evan said yes. He was hoping to get rid of his anxiety by exercising away his nervous energy—he didn't even care where the game was played!

That night, before the game began, both teams huddled together for prayer. Evan participated only because he wasn't sure how to abstain without seeming rude. During the game, he played with gusto and enjoyed himself immensely. When the game was over, he almost didn't mind participating in the closing prayer. However, when his co-worker invited him to return to the church for weekend services, Evan replied, "No thanks. God and I don't get along."

Of course his friend was curious and asked why not. The two men sat on the bleachers and

Evan poured out his story for the first time in almost
a year. At the end, he said, "If I knew where God
was, if I could find him right now... well, I'm
ashamed to tell you what I'd have to say to Him."
Evan's friend chuckled and said, "I'm sure He's
heard it all before. Go ahead."

"Go ahead and what?" Evan asked.

"Go ahead and have your say with God,"
said the friend, "He's right here. He's in this gym.
Tell him what you're feeling!"

Evan didn't know how to respond. Suddenly
uncomfortable and anxious, he quickly excused
himself and drove home. Once alone in his own
apartment, he gave into his frustrations. He yelled,
threw things, and ripped his daily newspaper and a
couple of magazines to shreds. And, then, he cried.
For the first time since the deaths of his loved ones,
Evan cried out *all* of his sorrow and fears. At some
point, in the midst of his emotional storm, Evan
began to talk to God; pouring out his heartbreak and
rage, fear and sadness. And, for the first time in a
long time, he was honest with God. "Right now, I
hate you!"

In the silence following his tumultuous rampage, Evan heard the voice of God. The Lord spoke, not in an audible way, but to Evan's broken heart. God poured out His love and compassion on Evan, like a waterfall of grace. In his heart, Evan felt the Spirit move and for the first time in a very long time, he knew peace.

We sometimes make the mistake of believing God leaves us when trouble comes. Just as oil and water can't mix, perhaps we make the assumption God and suffering can't be in the same room at the same time. We mistakenly believe if trouble comes into our life, God must have to leave it. Of course, nothing could be further from the truth.

It is in our weakness God is at His strongest!

### PRAYING TOGETHER

*Father, nothing and no one could be as close to us as you, even* and especially *in the midst of sorrow and pain. Teach us, Father, we can trust you to be as close as our own shadow during all the times of our lives, both good and bad. We pray this prayer in the name of your Son, Jesus Christ. Amen.*

## *JOURNALING YOUR THOUGHTS*

We can be certain, no matter what the circumstances, God will never leave us. He cares. In your journal today record your experiences of God's presence in your life.

Write about a time in your life when you could *not* feel God's presence.

Write about a time in your life when you were certain that God *was* by your side and working in your life.

What was different *about you* (if anything) from the first situation to the next?

# Psalms

Authored in part by King David (and in its entirety by many writers), the book of Psalms is a collection of memoirs, poetry, songs, and prayers. It was written to be used much in the same way we might use a collection of devotionals, study guides or even hymnbooks today—as a resource for enhancing our worship. The overwhelming theme of Psalms can be defined in just four words: God is in control.

# "I am what I am"

*[13] "For you created my innermost being; you knit me together in my mother's womb".*
*—Psalm 139:13*

Tammy and I were supposed to be on our way to a Christian women's conference in Dallas. However, Tammy was late picking me up—*as usual*. When she pulled up in front of my house (almost 40 minutes later than she said she would), I wasn't at all surprised by what she was wearing. She was sitting behind the wheel in a lovely white silk blouse, blue linen jacket, a broach, a pearl necklace, and high heels. But, where her skirt should have been, there was only a white silk slip! That should have shocked me, but it didn't. Let's just say Tammy is one skirt short of a full outfit.

I asked, "Skirt?"

She replied, "Dry cleaners."

"Naturally," said I.

She grinned. "I thought we'd stop on the way and pick it up. We have plenty of time."

For Tammy, time is always relative. I haven't the foggiest idea what it is relative *to*—her concept of time has absolutely no kinship to *my* concept of time. Yet, I've learned to live with this quirkiness in Tammy. "I am what I am," she says. And, she is!

We did indeed stop at the dry cleaners. Where she boldly stepped out of her car, in just her slip, and walked into the shop. I would have died a thousand deaths before I showed myself in public that way, but Tammy has no such inhibitions. She giggled at my shock and said, *"My slip is silk— expensive silk—and if I remember correctly, it cost more than the skirt, so why not show it off?"* She had a point. What she did not have was a skirt!

She came out of the dry cleaners, stood right beside the door of her minivan in the parking lot, removed her skirt from its protective plastic wrapping, and pulled it up and over her expensive silk slip. She took time to wave and smile pleasantly at several "lookie-loos" who, walking past her car stopped to stare, and at the shop owner who was laughing heartily from inside the dry-cleaners.

There's one thing you can say about Tammy: What you see is *literally* what you get. You'll never meet anyone more genuine than this lady. Tammy is a God-fearing, kind, loving, generous, wonderful *and* quirky human being. God may have created her to be a little more "out there" than the rest of us, but He also created her to be unique and genuine.

I find that last part—*unique and genuine*—to be very important.

There is no other human being on earth exactly like Tammy, or me *or you*. Even my twin cousins (Rodney and Ronald) are different, each from the other. They are unique as individuals with distinct likes and dislikes, opinions and feelings.

And, even though science says they are identical—born of one egg—still they are different. I find Ronald's eyes to be a tiny bit softer and kinder and Rodney's smile a tiny bit bigger and brighter. God planned it this way. He created each of us by hand; each of us as individual works of art, created by a master hand to be of genuine worth.

The best piece of advice I could ever give to others, and myself, is to allow yourself to retain the uniqueness God gave you before birth and to be **genuine**. Don't try to be someone you're not. We all have something that makes us different from everyone else around us. I'm told I have a slight accent—a *tiny* Texas twang—if that's what makes me different, then I'm going to embrace it!

Whatever it is that sets <u>you</u> apart— accept it! Share it! Revel in it! Let everyone around you see you for who and what you really are—the masterpiece God created you to be! Be genuine! Be you!

### *PRAYING TOGETHER*

*Father, you knew me when I was in my mother's womb and made me to be someone special! I am different than every other human being on earth. I have a purpose and a reason for being who I am. You, the Great "I AM" knew before I was ever born what characteristics, qualities, personality traits and experiences you wanted me to have in order for me to serve you. I praise you and thank you for making me truly unique and I ask for your help and the strength of character I need to be truly genuine. I pray Father, with love for You and your Son in my heart. Amen*

### *JOURNALING YOUR THOUGHTS*

It is sometimes hard to take a good long look at ourselves and decide whether we like what we see, or not. Sometimes, however, it is the very thing we need to do. It's time to evaluate! Spend some time today telling your journal how you really feel about, *you.* Answer two, three or all of the questions to give yourself a good handle on your feelings.

I like myself. True or false? Why or why not?

(Read Psalm 139) Do I believe the Word of God is good and true? If so, how could I ever question God's love for *me*?

The God of the universe, creator of heaven and earth took time to knit *me* together in my mother's womb. Shouldn't I be happy to be who he made me to be?

# Proverbs

Written mostly by King Solomon, the book of Proverbs is a collection of "truisms", common sense instructions for leading a righteous life. They cover a myriad of diverse subjects from child rearing to social justice. The overall theme of the book is a simple message, live rightly and justly in the eyes of the Lord and you will live well.

# Enjoy the Ride

*⁹We may make our own plans, but it is the LORD who decides where we will go.  —Proverbs 16:9*

From the air, the tiny island of Bermuda seems minuscule. Just twenty-six miles in length and averaging only one to two miles in width, it's hard to believe such a tiny piece of land is a *country*! Roads from one end of the island to the other are a twisted and tangled, winding mess. These highways and byways are so narrow you can stick your hand out the window of your moving vehicle and touch the cars traveling in the other direction. Of course, you would lose that hand because everyone in Bermuda drives 100 miles per hour everywhere they go! At least, it seems that way.

I'm not sure I've ever been as frightened in my life as I was sitting in the back of a Bermudian taxi during a vacation many years ago. The driver, a grinning, deeply-tanned, and jovial man who called himself "Singing Sam" careened around corners, almost on two wheels, and wildly zipped in and out of traffic like a madman. Riding in Sam's taxi was like being trapped on an out of control roller coaster while Elvis crooned "Blue Suede Shoes" from the forward seat.

The most frightening part of the ride was the way Sam came upon other vehicles in front of him, waiting until the last possible moment to slam on his brakes. He missed the bumpers of other vehicles by what seemed like only inches. Even Lester (the hubster), a normally unflappable and stoic passenger, was unnerved and looked slightly nauseated.

Luckily, afterwards we were able to walk most everywhere we went. However, three days into our stay Lester decided to rent a motor scooter. He wanted to see the whole country. He surmised we could drive from one end of the island to the other, riding double, without having to rely on any of the wildly dangerous taxicabs. It was a good idea *in theory*.

I have to tell you though; I hated the scooter almost as much as Sam's cab. I loathed the feeling of being so out-of-control—and so close to death! I had no power over the way my husband drove the mini-bike. Just as I'd had no control over the way Sam had driven his taxi, or how the other drivers on the road maneuvered their vehicles. I had no real control over whether I lived or died while in Bermuda or... in truth... any day before or since. It's a terrifying thought, knowing I'm not really in command of my life.

Sadly, it's only human nature to want the dominion over our lives to be in our own hands; it's hard to give power away to anyone, even God. However, we can trust there is no one more qualified to lead our steps and direct our fate than Him. Our own efforts to manipulate our destiny only leave us careening out of control. We have to trust in God to get us safely from one end of our trip to the other.

*⁵Trust in the Lord with all of your heart; do not depend on your own understanding. ⁶Seek his will in all you do, and he will direct your paths.*
*—Proverbs 3:5-6*

Although giving up control of my life to the Lord is sometimes hard to do, I do it because I trust Him. If you haven't yet handed over your life to God, maybe now is the time to do so. Let Him decide which way to go and how to get there. Let Him decide to turn left or right, to take the job or not, to get married or move on, or to say yes or no. It's not as terrifying as it may sound. No one *on earth* is more qualified than God to be in control of your life—not even you. So, sit back and enjoy the ride. Trust God!

### PRAYING TOGETHER

*Heavenly God, how exciting this trip we call life can be! The twists and turns we experience on winding, tangled roads leave us confused, trembling*

*and afraid. Yet, with you in the driver's seat, we can*
*trust we'll reach our destination safe and happy. Be*
*patient with us, Father, as we learn to trust in you*
*and let go of the control we think we have over our*
*lives. Teach us trust in the notion that you direct*
*our paths. Once we realize that, our trip will be*
*much more enjoyable. I pray in the name of your*
*Son, Jesus Christ, the Returning Savior. Amen.*

### *JOURNALING YOUR THOUGHTS*

Giving control of our lives to anyone else is terrifying. Yet, God not only asks that of us, He expects it. Trust is a verb—it takes action to prove our love and faith in Him. Write today about your experiences trusting God.

Have you given God complete control over your life? Why or why not?

When you retain control, do things turn out the way you wanted them to?

What might have happened if you had gone to God instead?

# Ecclesiastes

Though the authorship of Ecclesiastes is uncertain, it is generally accepted the writer was most likely King Solomon who may have written it after trying to live apart from God. The author begins this book with a series of detailed descriptive warnings about the things men should *not* do with their lives. He explains his own foolhardiness in ignoring God and his fellow man. Though he is the possessor of wealth, wisdom and welcoming friends he soon discovers only God can fill the void in his heart. Following this epiphany, the book ends with proverb-like sayings and truths describing the futility of living a life without the Lord.

# The Tie that Binds

*[12]Though one may be overpowered two can defend themselves. A cord of three strands is not quickly broken. —Ecclesiastes 4:12*

I was a Campfire girl when I was very young.

I am remembering a time when our troop was learning how to tie all sorts of different knots in rope. As we sat in a circle, we were each given a six-foot section of cord to practice with; it was thick, heavy rope almost too big for our tiny hands to use. I remember being bored stiff, until…

On our own, waiting outside to be picked up by our parents after the meeting, we began playing with those sections of twine. We lassoed one another, and jump-roped; some of us broke off into pairs and tied ourselves to the ends of our rope sections. Then we played tug-of-war by pulling away from our partners with the lash holding us together at the middle. We had a ton of fun trying to topple one another, pulling against each other until sweat popped out on our foreheads. Then, sometimes on purpose, we fell on top of one another laughing and giggling. We ran around the yard squealing and screaming tangling the ropes intentionally. It was a blast!

Those twisted jute cords took a beating that afternoon but not one of them broke.

That's how it is with God's love. He acts as the tie binding us in marriage, in friendship, and in relationships between parents and children. He stands in the gap between us and those we love tightly holding on to both ends, never letting go. His bond is unbreakable!

Like my husband and I, many of you have invited the Lord to be a part of your marriage—to be the tie that binds. But, have you asked Him to enter into your other relationships, as well? Have you asked Him to be a part of your friendships with your neighbors and coworkers; to strengthen the relationship between you and your children, your parents or your in-laws?

Whenever someone new comes into my life—a friend, a neighbor, a coworker or family member—I ask God to bind us together. His strength and determination to make the relationship strong reinforces my own efforts. Before too long, my friend and I are part of a triple-braided cord that cannot be broken. God's binding love will strengthen any and all of your relationships in the same way, but you have to ask Him to tie the knot.

If you have not yet invited the Lord into your relationships—*all of them*—maybe it's time to do so. For one alone can be defeated. Two together can conquer. But, three standing together back-to-back, fortified and strong, are invincible! Ask God to be the tie that binds you and everyone you know and love. You'll be glad you did!

### PRAYING TOGETHER

*Father, you are so strong. Without your strength to bind me to those I love, I would fall apart. My relationships might falter. My ties would be broken. Only with your help can I keep my bonds with others unbreakable. Father, I ask you to come into every relationship I make and bind me to those I care about. I ask you to stand in the gap between us. I ask this of you because I know you will honor a request made in your will. I ask in the name of Jesus, amen.*

### JOURNALING YOUR THOUGHTS

Is God a part of *every* relationship in your life? Is God on the inside binding you and yours close together? Or, is He on the outside looking in at a breakable or fraying attachment? Take a moment to jot some thoughts into your journal about your different relationships and how they could be improved by God's active participation.

I have (or have not) asked God into all of my relationships. Why or why not?

God's active presence in my relationship(s) has resulted in the following changes:

I have a strained relationship with _____. Would asking God to stand in the gap between us help the situation? How?

# Song of Songs

Think of this book of the Bible as the written script
to an opera. It includes a male lead, a female lead
and a chorus. It is a highly stylized narrative
describing the longing between a man and his
beloved, the struggles they face and the joy they
find in one another's arms. Although many find the
subject matter somewhat controversial, it is
included in the Bible, some say, as a symbolic
interpretation of the joy found in the love between
God and his church.

# When a Man
# Loves a Woman

*⁴ Take me away with you—let us hurry!*
*Let the king bring me into his chambers.*
*—Song of Songs 1:4*

How sweet is the passion between a husband
and wife who truly love one another? It is sweeter

than the finest wine—so says the story of Solomon's love for his beloved. Many read this portion of God's Word, the Song of Songs, and assign to it a symbolic meaning. For example, some say this book is all about God's love for His people, the Israelites. Some say it is symbolic of Christ's love for His entire church.

Me? I tend to take a more literal view of the Song of Songs. I believe it is simply a story about a man's love for the woman who stirs his passion. In other words, it's all about sex.

When I told my husband I'd be writing about sex today, he rolled his eyes and said, "Don't do it!"

Sex is such a touchy subject among believers—especially women. Some take a very solid stand against it. (Never mind the perpetuation of the species simply could not continue without it.) In years past, some ladies have seen sex as a chore and something we, as women, simply *must* do—like washing dishes and folding laundry. As you can imagine this attitude has provided comics *and husbands* with hours of stand-up material.

When Meredith Vieira was co-host of the
Today Show, she once poked fun at ladies who feel
so strongly about their "duty" in this fashion and
told this joke: *"An elderly woman gathered her
seven children to her side as she lay on her
deathbed and said, 'I'm proud to say that I'm going
to die a virgin.' Her seven children looked at one
another and then at her and said, 'Mom, how can
that be? You have seven children. You had to have
had sex at least seven times in your life.' The old
woman responded, 'Yes, but I didn't participate.'"*

Gladly, times have changed. Few women
still feel that way. For many of us married women,
the passion we share with our husbands is more like
a much-beloved hobby than a chore. That cherished
time alone with our mates is something we look
forward to, dream about, and romanticize. It's a
time of communion between two souls who care
deeply and passionately for each other. (Sometimes,
it's just about celebrating each time the kids are out
of the house long enough for us to be alone!)

Can I be honest with you? I've never been a
big fan of this particular book of the Bible.
Although I am very comfortable with my own

intimate relationship, I've never been as comfortable hearing about someone else's. Don't get me wrong. I'm not a prude. I'm just not comfortable in the role of Peeping-Tom. So, the Song of Songs has always seemed *to me* to be strangely out-of-place in the Bible. However, even I have to admit its message is valid. Physical love between a husband and wife is meant to be good and holy.

Although I'm not comfortable seeing or reading about the sex lives of others, I'm grateful for my own loving relationship with a man whose only thought is to make me feel loved. *He* is a gift from God.

I am thankful for the openness with which God shares his love for us through the pages of His Word. I hope to one day grow to love the Song of Songs because its message is worth knowing. It is a beautiful description of love between a man and wife. It is also a stunning way to view these truths—*God created love. God sustains love. God Is Love.*

## *PRAYING TOGETHER*

*My God, what an awesome display of love you have shared with us through Your Word. You have shown us through lyric and song how wonderful loving devotion can be. The passion shared between a husband and wife is truly a gift. It can be more than just intimate. It can be spiritual. You have shown love by gifting love. Father I thank you.*

*I pray in the name of Your Son, the epitome of love. Amen*

## *JOURNALING YOUR THOUGHTS*

Loving, caring, passionate and intimate encounters with our spouses are certainly something to be celebrated. Yet, in the fast-paced, crowded world we live in, those encounters can sometimes be few and far between. So, how do we keep the spark alive?

Spend some time today coming up with ideas to "spark" some romance in your marriage. Remember—passion isn't always all about fireworks. Sometimes it's about cherishing the presence of your partner in your life—and making sure they know it!

# Isaiah

Isaiah was a prophet God sent to Judah the Southern portion of Israel (although many of his prophecies covered the northern kingdom as well). He experienced the terrible civil war between the two principalities, first hand. He also saw the destruction of Israel by the Assyrians in 722 B.C. With careful study one will notice Jesus quotes the book of Isaiah often simply because its overall theme is one of rescue and restoration.

# Twinkle, Twinkle

*26Lift up your eyes and look to the heavens. Who created all these? He who brings out the starry host one by one, and calls forth each of them by name. Because of his great power and mighty strength, not one of them is missing. —Isaiah 40:26*

"Mama what's his name?" I looked around to see who Katie, my four-year-old daughter, might be asking about. We were surrounded by people, all of us waiting for the July Fourth fireworks to begin.

My husband and I had chosen a spot high on a hill overlooking the ball fields to watch the show. Dozens of families, like ours, were sitting nearby in lawn chairs and on blankets.

"Who, baby?" I asked, "Who are you talking about?"

She sighed in frustration and pointed straight up, "What's *his* name; the one in the middle, the one that's winking at me?"

"Oh! I don't think stars have names, honey."

Again, she sighed, a testament in patience towards my stupidity. "Yes they do. Everything has a name, mama. What's *his* name?"

I glanced at my husband who just smiled and shrugged at me. I looked back at Katie and said, "Oh, *that one*! His name is Joe."

"Joe," she said, "Stop winking at me. It's not nice!"

Many years later during a Bible study session, I thought of Joe.

Session leader Audrey had asked, "Do you feel God's love in your life, day-to-day?" Most of us very quickly said yes and several went on to give examples of how God's love had impacted their lives *that* day. However, Janet didn't respond until prodded by Audrey.

Very reluctantly she said, "I don't doubt God's love for me as one of His children. I *do* doubt he checks in on me, or any of you, daily. We're part of a huge crowd made up of billions on this earth. There is nothing about our boring little lives that would catch His attention—at least not on a daily basis."

A debate ensued lasting several *lo-o-o-ng* moments. It ended only when we all agreed to disagree. However, before the end of the session, Audrey said, "I just remembered a scripture I'd like to share with you, Janet." She shared Isaiah 40:26.

Sadly, I don't think Audrey and the rest of us ever truly convinced Janet God does indeed love her—daily. Even more sadly, Janet isn't the first person I've heard question her worth, as an individual, in God's eyes. I once overheard a conversation in which the speaker said, "Jesus died for sinners as a group—it was a blanket sacrifice, meant to cover all of us, for all sins. My day-to-day goofs aren't even on His radar."

If a blanket sacrifice had been sufficient to cover everyone's sins, from petty jealousies to vicious murder, God could have just sent *a goat*, a big goat perhaps, but just a goat. However, that's not what happened. It took much more than the death of a lowly sin-eater to cleanse the sins of *all* people.

My sin, your sin, his sin, her sin, our sin *as individuals* is what kept us separated from God. Only a **precious** sacrifice, one that would be keenly felt, would suffice to save us *by name* from the darkness of eternity. Only the death of His Son would give us eternal life. How small minded it is to believe that that kind of sacrifice would be given so cheaply as to cover all mankind like a blanket.

God sent His Son to die for us; not a goat or an ox or an elephant but his Son, because He loves each one of us. Separately and uniquely, He loves us—as individuals.

If a four-year-old little girl can recognize one star, out of billions, and call it by name, how easy it must be for God to recognize each of us, call us by name, and then cover us each in the blood of Jesus and wash us white as snow.

Never believe, for even one second, God does not know your name or hear your prayers each and every day. He gave His Only Son for you! He loves YOU!

## *PRAYING TOGETHER*

*Father, Abba, I sit here this day with tears in my eyes wondering at your awesome love. How grateful I am you thought of me, as an individual, when you sent your Son to die for the sins of mankind. How grateful I am to You, Jesus, and how awed I am you would do what you did, for me. For ME. You love me. No matter how unworthy I am, My God, I give my life to you—daily. I pray in the name of Jesus Christ, my Returning Savior. Amen*

## *JOURNALING YOUR THOUGHTS*

God in heaven *is* God, the King of the Universe. Yet, each day and all through the night, He looks down from His lofty place and loves <u>*you*</u>! Record in your journal today your thoughts about God's love for *you* as an individual

True or false: I believe God loves me and is a part of my daily life. Choose one and explain why you feel the way you do.

Believing God sent His Son as a sacrifice for our individual sins makes that sacrifice more uniquely personal. Explain how that might make a difference in your life concerning your own sinful nature.

# Jeremiah

Jeremiah could be considered the best known of the biblical prophets simply because he was described in such detail in this book. He lived during the last forty years Judah was a nation—before the fall to Babylon. He was witness to the slaughter of his people and the enslavement of the survivors and he saw Solomon's grand temple fall. He knew it all to be the judgment of God. He begged the Israelites to turn from their sins and return to righteousness in God's eyes.

# Cracked Pots

*"For my people have committed two evils; they have forsaken me the fountain of living waters, and hewed them out cisterns, broken cisterns, that can hold no water."* —Jeremiah 2:13

I love antiques. I have several in my home of which I'm very proud, including a 100-year-old Bible that belonged to my husband's grandfather, a century-old sled and an ancient toddler's chair that was hewn from wood at least 100 years ago. However, I am by no means an expert on antiques.

That ignorance can sometimes get me into trouble.

Many years ago, a very good friend of mine invited several of us over for dinner.

Betty's home is beautiful—beautiful enough to be on a magazine cover. So, after the meal, several of us wandered through the house "oohing" and "ahhing". I personally had never seen so many lovely things outside of a museum.

However, most of us were surprised to come across a rusty-looking greenish metal lantern on Betty's fireplace mantel next to several beautiful cut crystal pieces. The lantern inspired a hastily covered "yuck" from me. It was so out of place.

"Betty," I said, "Tell me about this lamp."

Betty excitedly explained she had just acquired the brass ship's lantern the week before. Supposedly, it was from a shipwrecked vessel off the British Virgin Islands. She was obviously quite proud of it.

My distaste must have been evident because Betty scowled and asked if I liked it. I made the mistake of being honest, "I suppose if the ugly green stuff could be polished off the shiny brass, it might be pretty."

Imagine my surprise at the look of pure horror crossing Betty's face. "The green patina is what makes it beautiful and proves it's antique!"

AKWARD!

Several years later, I came across on article entitled "Instant Patina for Brass." According to the author, it was very easy to achieve a green patina on brass by employing a small amount of ammonia, regular table salt, a hand-held hair dryer, plus a little bit of patience. What looked brand new on Tuesday could look hundreds of years old by Wednesday. I was reminded of Betty's antique ship's lantern. Had it really come from the sea? Or had it come to her via the local do-it-yourself-depot with a short stop-over in a bath of ammonia and salt? I'll never know…and I would never tell Betty even if I did!

We can often be fooled by the fakes and phonies of this world. So many of us are led astray by people my dad calls "cracked pots"—psychics, get-rich-quick artists, con-men, and televangelists who aren't as sincere in their worship of God as they are in their worship of money and lusts.

Through the prophet Jeremiah, God said:

*"For my people have committed two evils; they have forsaken me the fountain of living waters, and hewed them out cisterns, broken cisterns, that can hold no water." –Jeremiah 2:13*

When we put our faith into those who might be fakes and phonies, we're pouring our spirits into cracked pots. If a crack develops in a cistern, the water seeps away into the surrounding dirt and is lost forever. Don't make the mistake of falling for a fake or a phony. God alone is worthy!

### *PRAYING TOGETHER*

*Adonai! Glorious God, you alone are worthy of our praise and adulation! You alone are worthy! We worship you as the One True God. Father, open our eyes to your value in our lives. Help us to see the fallacy of the enemy's message that anything else could ever be substituted in our*

*lives for you. You alone are our treasure. We pray
in the name of your precious Son, Amen.*

### *JOURNALING YOUR THOUGHTS*

God's Word is the only authentic antique
worth investing in! Do not forsake His Living
Water or pour your spirit into a broken cistern that
isn't worthy of holding it! Using all or just some of
the prompts below, (or) allow your mind to wander
free, to journal your feelings about how *well* your
relationship with God is holding.

Think of random words or thoughts; or draw
pictures on the subject of God and/or your
relationship with Him. Doodle them in your journal.
As you go, your thoughts will become more solid
and defined. Go with the flow. This is called Free
Association. It will help you to more fully define
your feelings. Use the following examples to get
you started.

- ❖ CRACKED
- ❖ PERFECTION
- ❖ EMPTY
- ❖ FILLED

- ❖ HURTING
- ❖ JOYFUL
- ❖ KNOCKED OVER
- ❖ STANDING TALL

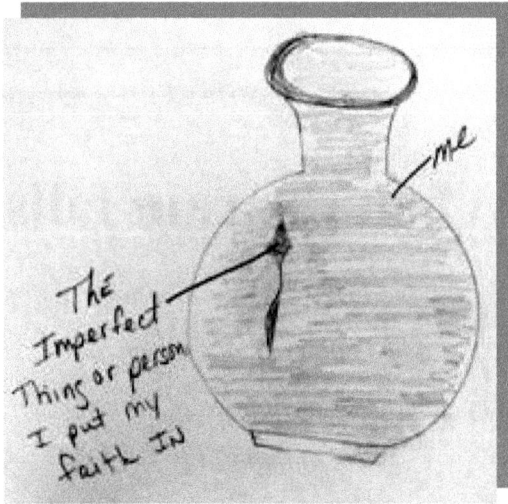

# Lamentations

True to its name, the book of Lamentations is full of woe and misery. Written by the prophet Jeremiah, after the fall of Solomon's Holy Temple and all of Jerusalem, it is a funeral dirge for the nation of Israel. Lamentations is a painful reminder to all… God *does* punish sins. However, He is a forgiving God and His compassion never fails.

# When the rain falls

*[22] Because of the LORD's great love we are not consumed, for his compassions never fail [23] they are new every morning; great is your faithfulness.*
*—Lamentations 3: 22-23*

When my oldest daughter, Katie, went off to college, I expected her to come home with homework, laundry, and maybe a boyfriend or two. I never expected her to come home with a dog! Although he was as cute as a bug, Charlie was the funniest looking little puppy I'd ever seen. He was low to the ground and shaped just like his mother, a Daschund. However, his coloring and ears came from his daddy, the blue heeler.

Charlie and I didn't get along at first. As a matter of fact, Charlie didn't get along with anyone, but Katie. Before Katie's first spring break was over he'd bitten each of the rest of us at least once. None of us was sad to see him go back to school with her.

The next year, when Lester and I and our other two kids, moved to Las Vegas, and left Katie behind to continue her education, I wasn't too worried about her safety. With Charlie around I believed her to be in good hands ... er, paws.

Just a few months later, however, Katie decided to leave school and move to Nevada with the rest of us. She and Charlie made the 1200-mile trip and moved in to stay, for a while.

Unfortunately, Charlie's personality had not changed one bit in the interim. He was still a mean little cuss and a biter.

For some reason he especially didn't like the Hubster, Lester. Every time Lester came near his daughter—even to just pass her in the hallway—Charlie tore into him! Lester became infuriated just having the dog in the house! My mantra became, "He's only here until she can find a place of her own".

Imagine Lester's dismay (and mine) when Katie did find a place of her own—*that wouldn't allow pets*! She begged us to keep Charlie for her until her circumstances changed. Lester said, "NO WAY, NO HOW!" But, by then, Baylie, our youngest, *lonesome and home-sick for Texas*, had latched on to Charlie as if he was a life-preserver and she was drowning at sea.

Lester wanted the dog gone. The girls wanted him to stay. They all wanted me to choose one side over the other. My house became a war zone with me caught in the middle.

I took my dilemma to my new Prayer Warrior and friend, Joan, who actually prayed for Charlie. She said, "I've never prayed for a dog before, but I know God will make Charlie calm down if we ask him." Would you believe it worked? Charlie never bit Lester, or any of us, again! We *all* began to fall in love with the new and improved Charlie! He became a loving and gentle member of the family showing just what prayer really can do!

In June of 2008, when Charlie was six years old, something changed in him. He stopped playing, stopped smiling (yes, he smiled) and stopped eating. He began vomiting almost every day. It became very evident very quickly he was ill. In less than two weeks, he grew so weak he began to have a hard time walking.

Of course we took him to the vet. The news was terrible. His entire little weenie-shaped body was eaten up with cancer. The decision was made to end his suffering and put him to sleep. In the end, it was over very quickly for Charlie but the rest of us were in pain for quite a while. We had come to love him greatly over time.

My mother sometimes says, "Into every life a little rain must fall." There will be times when each of us will suffer a loss like this—or one that hits with greater magnitude. A family member will pass, a job will end, a friend will be lost, or a marriage will dissolve. These things are painful. It is in these moments when we can rely most on God. His compassion never fails!

He understands our pain and confusion and grief. He understands because He, too, experienced those things through the life of Jesus. When Lazarus died—even though Jesus knew, with God's power, Lazarus would be raised again—*he wept*. He grieved. He suffered loss and pain.

God understands our hurts. In our time of grief He will hold us and comfort us and mourn with us until the time comes to laugh again. The Bible says:

*[18]The LORD is close to the brokenhearted and saves those crushed in spirit. —Psalm 34:18*

Are you crushed in spirit? Are you broken hearted? Remember, when the rain falls… God will be your umbrella!

### *PRAYING TOGETHER*

*Father in Heaven you are so worthy to be praised. No one, no human being, could ever comfort us or love us to the extent that you can; if we will only allow ourselves to fall into your arms and be loved by you… I praise you Father for your*

*compassions that never fail! In the name of your*
*Son who loved us enough to be one of us, Amen*

### *JOURNALING YOUR THOUGHTS*

God understands your pain and loss. When
Eve took what was forbidden and started the human
race on a downward spiral that continues to this
day—God's grief began. Every day he mourns the
loss of another soul, another sin, another denial of
Him. He understands your pain. Write in your
journal today about your feelings on loss.

In times of trouble and pain I always turn
first to _____.

*Why?*

If your answer above was not "God", what
keeps you from his throne room when you're in
pain?

# Ezekiel

A Jewish priest, a member of the tribe of Levi, and a Babylonian captive, Ezekiel also became a prophet of God when he foretold the complete destruction of Judah (the southern kingdom of Israel). His prophecy came to pass earning him respect among the people of Israel. He became their sentinel against immoral living and the wages of sin.

# It's all About Me...
# or, is it?

*49 " 'Now this was the sin of your sister Sodom: She and her daughters* [Gomorrah & the surrounding villages] *were arrogant, overfed and unconcerned; they did not help the poor and needy. 50 They were haughty and did detestable things before me. Therefore, I did away with them as you have seen' ".*
—*Ezekiel 16:49-50*

Turning thirty was traumatic for me (however, now that I've passed the age of forty and am closing in on fifty I can't remember why). It was a hard birthday for me to *celebrate*. I just couldn't stomach the thought of celebrating *old age*. (How naïve was I?)

At the time, a very good friend said to me, "Honey, I thought I'd die when I turned thirty, too!" She offered to take me to a local spa for some good old-fashioned pampering, showing me a brochure describing all the amenities to which she wanted to treat me to:

1.  a full manicure including moisturizing, stripping and shearing the cuticle;

2.  a complete pedicure with heel scraping;

3.  A full facial integrating an eyebrow wax and a yogurt-pea gravel cleansing rub (huh?);

4.  And a chin and upper lip threading, which, I'm told, yanks the facial hair right out by the root using sewing thread (yippee!).

The package also included a steam bath, hot rock massage, and optional acupuncture.

Paula described the entire procedure as the *height of self-indulgence*. It sounded more like torture to me, but what do I know? My idea of self-indulgent activity involves a good book and a quiet room.

Every woman—*every person*—has a different inspiration for self-indulgence. Although I have never been keen on the idea of strangers poking me with needles, weighing me down with hot rocks, or even touching my feet; I've also never been one to neglect any opportunity to spoil, pamper, or coddle myself in other ways.

For example, I rarely shop for others without purchasing something for myself, as well. And the generous suggestion to my husband, "Why don't you go play a round of golf—you deserve it" is usually just a tactic to get the house to myself so I can take a long bath and watch movies alone. It's my own brand of hedonism!

While some may argue self-indulgence is okay every once in a while, it is the whole-hearted approach to self-interest (as was seen in Sodom before her destruction) that prompted Ezekiel's harsh rebuke and warning which we see in today's scripture.

There is nothing wrong with treating yourself to a long bath, or good book, or even helping yourself to a day of torture at a spa. However, God expects us to put the needs of others ahead of ourselves as often as possible. (*Heb. 13:16, Prov. 22:9, Luke 6:38, 1 John 3:17, Matt 25:35-40, plus many more*)

As a result of my own study concerning this topic, I've made a commitment to myself to be less aware of my own wants and wishes and more proactive when thinking of others—inside and outside of my home.

In other words, I'm actively searching for ways to serve others. At home, I've begun doing little things to help ease my husband's burden. For example, although I hate working outdoors I've begun weeding each morning as I wait with my grandson for the school bus. I'm taking out the trash more and sweeping off the porch, all things he used to do. And, whenever I find my daughter's laundry in the dryer, I fold it for her. I've even begun washing the dishes when it's her turn...well, I've done it twice. I started doing dozens of tiny things for my family like this, helping when and where I can. It may not sound like a lot. But, every little thing I do for them places them before me. *And*, my family and I have committed to donate goods, services and time to our local charity at least once a month. It's a start.

The Apostle Paul said it best:

> *⁴Let each of you look out not only for his own interests, but also for the interests of others.*
> —*Philippians 2:4 (**NKJV**)*

If pleasing God is the end result of watching my self-indulgent calorie count, then I think it's high time I went on a diet. Don't you?

Spend some time in prayer this week and ask God to help *you* to go on a self-indulgence diet. It will do you—and others—a whole lot of good!

### PRAYING TOGETHER

*Father in heaven, I worship you as the God of generosity and giving. I ask that you will grow in me the desire to do more for my fellow man.*

*Diminish me in my own sight. Raise up in me the*
*will and the power to do for and be for others what*
*they need from me. I ask, essentially, to be more like*
*Your Son, Jesus. I pray these things with the*
*boldness He gave to me, Amen.*


### *JOURNALING YOUR THOUGHTS*

Use one or more of the prompts below to
help you find a way to actively apply the principle
of today's devotional.


What am I willing to do to make myself
more aware of others *daily*?


Make a list and choose one or all of your
options to put into practice.


Write a poem, haiku, song lyrics, a story or
just a paragraph about thoughtfulness *or* self-
indulgence to describe how you'd like your life to
be from this point forward.

# Daniel

Daniel grew up a Hebrew captive in Babylon. Favored by those in power, he was educated by his captors and indoctrinated into, and rose quickly through the ranks of, the Babylonian government. However, throughout his captivity Daniel and three of his friends (Shadrach, Meshach and Abednego) held steadfastly to their Jewish faith. Refusing to bow down before the created gods of Babylon they were arrested, judged and sentenced to death. Daniel was thrown into a den of lions and the others were placed in a fiery furnace. However, all four survived their ordeals untouched proving the power, mercy and grace of the one true God.

# Even If

*"But even if He does not [save us], we want you to know, O king; we will not serve your gods or worship the image of gold you have set up."*
*—Daniel 3:18*

Too many times in the history of Christianity, believers have been forced to face an almost impossible decision—give up their faith or give up their lives. However, I would imagine in that penultimate moment, all of them **hoped** God would save them from having to suffer a horrible death. Yet, each of them in those final moments knew while God *could* save them, He might choose not to. They knew, as Jesus once knew, their deaths might serve a greater purpose than their lives ever could.

However, there have been others who have escaped their predicaments with both their faith and their heads intact.

For example: Shadrach, Meshach and Abednego were three young Hebrew captives in Babylon who were given a very serious choice: Bow down before the golden idol of the Babylonian king, Nebuchadnezzar, or forfeit their lives in a fiery furnace. Their answer came swiftly and with zeal.

*16 Shadrach, Meshach and Abednego replied to him, "King Nebuchadnezzar, we do not need to defend ourselves before you in this matter.* [17] *If we are thrown into the blazing furnace, the God we serve is able to deliver us from it, and he will deliver us from Your Majesty's hand.* [18] *But even if he does not, we want you to know, Your Majesty, that we will not serve your gods or worship the image of gold you have set up."* —*Daniel 3:16-18*

My heart pounds every time I read this passage. I'm so impressed by the courage and fierceness of faith Shadrach, Meshach and Abednego possessed. They believed with all of their hearts the Lord would save them from the flames. They believed with ferocity God would swoop down from heaven and rescue them. They believed God would save them from the furnace in a glorious showing of supernatural derring-do, bringing glory to His name and purpose to their faith.

And yet, there were those two little words… *"even if"*.

Even if God never arrived, even if they perished in the fire, even if there were no angels, no miracles, and no fireworks from heaven on their behalf… *even if,* they would not bow down. They would not give up. They would not give away their faith, God's glory, or His renown. *Even if.*

In the face of their inspirational faith, I have to ask myself if I have that same courage. When faced with illness, death, loss, and pain, do I have the guts to say to God, *"even if"*? Do you?

### PRAYING TOGETHER

*Heavenly Father, create in me a desire to bend to your will. Give me the courage and the tenacity to face whatever comes my way with the knowledge that you will save me—one way or another. Give me the strength to say, "even if" with confidence—no matter the furnace I may find myself in. I love you, Lord. Amen*

### JOURNALING YOUR THOUGHTS

It isn't easy learning to trust in God when you don't understand His plan. It takes practice, patience and preparation. Follow one or more of the suggestions below to help your exercise and strengthen your "even if" muscles—journal your results.

In your current situation(s), it may be hard to say *even if,* because of fear and doubt. In your journal, list the reasons you're feeling insecure and anxious. THEN, read Isaiah 41:13.

Does this passage give you hope? Record your thoughts.

Does it allay your fears? If not, why not? Record your reasons.

Research scriptures which might help you fight your fears.

Ask others to pray for you.

Pray today, and every day, that God will strengthen your "even if" muscles. Record your prayers.

# Hosea

Before the fall of the northern kingdom of Israel in 722 B.C., Hosea was a prophet there. The Lord spoke directly to Hosea and urged him to marry a certain prostitute, an amoral woman named Gomer. God used Hosea's marriage as an illustration to the people of His own love for them. Even though they ran from His love (just as Gomer ran from Hosea) and did deplorable things—sacrificing to unspeakable gods—he loved them anyway.

# Push Me, Pull You

*[2] But the more they were called, the more they went away from me. ... —Hosea 11:2a*

Eileen was devastated when her teenaged son came to her and her husband and said, "I'm gay. I've met someone. His name is Liam, and we're moving to New York together. We can be ourselves there."

When she was able to breathe again, Eileen said, "I think we should pray as a family". Jason, her son, replied, "No. I don't think I believe in God any more. Christian gay bashers make God seem cruel and hateful." Later she told her friends, "Jason telling us he's gay was the least upsetting thing he said. When he told me he didn't believe in God, my heart stopped beating."

When the shock wore off, Jim, Eileen's husband yelled, thumped his Bible, and argued with Jason until the boy ran off, swearing never to return. It was a terrifying situation for loving parents to live through. For a very long while, Eileen and Jim had no idea where Jason was living. Eventually, they discovered he had indeed moved to New York, with Liam.

Unfortunately, Jim's fear, anger and hurt found an outlet in the form of ugly letters and upsetting phone calls to his son. Jim preached *at* Jason blasting the boy with scripture and demanding repentance. On more than one occasion, he called his son names and said horrible things he could never take back. As far as Jason was concerned, Jim was acting like a horrible father...*and* a horrible Christian. After one particularly dreadful phone call, the two stopped communicating again, completely.

However, Eileen kept in touch with her son. She refused to allow a wall to be built between them. Still, she was heartbroken the two most important men in her life could not get along.

For five long years, Jason, Eileen, Jim and daughter Jill missed out on the joys of spending holidays, birthdays and special occasions together. Jill graduated from high school, and her brother missed the event. Jim and Eileen celebrated thirty years of marriage, and Jason wasn't there. Jill was married and her brother missed it. The rift between father and son had destroyed their family unit.

Years of tension caused the two women caught in the middle to reach their limit. *Somehow*, they persuaded Jim and Jason to meet face-to-face during a session with a Christian family counselor. The counselor shared with the family the story of Hosea.

Hosea's wife, Gomer, was not who Hosea wanted her to be; she was a prostitute who moved from party to party and man to man. Because of this, Hosea couldn't be certain his children really were *his* children. Gomer's lifestyle hurt him deeply and humiliated him in front of his whole town. However, since God had chosen Gomer to be his wife, Hosea would not divorce her.

God used Hosea's situation as an illustration for his people. Even when they chose to live in a way He didn't approve of—as Hosea didn't approve of his wife's lifestyle—He, loved them anyway.

The lesson was a strong one for Jim and Jason. They learned they could not force their opinions or lifestyles on one another. Yet, they could *and should* continue to love one another. The situation was not resolved that day, but eventually a dialogue began between father and son.

We love our children, family and friends. Seeing them make decisions we see as harmful to them is painful. We want to shake our loved ones and shout, "What are you thinking?" In my own experiences, I've discovered doing so just makes things worse; it just pushes away the very ones I'm trying so hard to hold on to.

Even God experienced this phenomenon when He said of Israel,

*11 "When Israel was a child, I loved him, and out of Egypt I called my son. 2 But the more they were called, the more they went away from me. They sacrificed to the Baals and they burned incense to images." —Hosea 11: 1-2*

We are certainly entitled to our opinions. And, we should share them, in a loving and caring way with those we love. Having done so, however, we then need to hand the situation over to God and allow Him to do the rest. When we find ourselves torn between hating a loved one's decision and loving them anyway, we need to go for the love every time. *That's* what Jesus would do.

### PRAYING TOGETHER

*Father, help us to look past those things that hurt us concerning our loved ones. Help us to learn to love them anyway, just as you love us despite our many faults and sins. We pray in the name of forgiveness, Jesus the Christ, Amen.*

## *JOURNALING YOUR THOUGHTS*

In today's story, Jason's sins were the only ones his father could see. However, if Jim had looked within he would have seen fear, hatred, bigotry and a very unforgiving spirit. Look into your heart today. Spend a few minutes journaling about your own experiences.

When I see a loved one making a decision about their life I see as being wrong or harmful, how do I approach the situation?

Do I use loving words and scripture to state my case or do I just explode?

How would Jesus handle these same situations?

Do I really care?  Or, do I just want to be right?

# Joel

This stirring account of prophecy has a simple message for the people of Jerusalem *and* future generations: heed God's warning or face destruction.

# Warning Signs

[1] *"Blow the trumpet in Zion; sound the alarm on my holy hill. Let all who live in the land tremble, for the day of the LORD is coming. It is close at hand..."*
—Joel 2:1

The first day of cool, soft rain was calming and peaceful. However, by the time the seventh day of hard rain began, I told my husband if he didn't *do something* to get us out of the house, I'd go crazy.

He was watching a weather alert on the television warning against unnecessary travel and gestured towards the television. I ignored him and said, "It can't be that bad. Let's go!"

The trip into Fort Worth was definitely an adventure. The normal half-hour drive to the mall took instead just over two hours. No matter; we were thrilled to be out of the house. We spent several hours wandering around the almost empty mall. Then, when we could see no more, we loaded up the car and headed home.

We were stopped by a police barricade not far from the mall. As we waited in a long line of cars, a policeman came to the window and told us the streets ahead of us were flooded and we should consider going back home. We explained we *were* headed home and told him where we lived. He suggested we rent a hotel room for the night. We ignored him; we turned around and sought another route.

Just a few streets from home we came to a small bridge which crosses over an ordinarily dry creek bed. We had to cross it; it was the only way to get home. But, the water level was so high, we couldn't even see it. My husband got out of the car and walked to the edge of the bridge to survey the situation. The water came up to his knees.

"As you know," he said when he came back to the car, "there is no other way home. Either we cross this bridge or we go back into town and find a place to stay." We decided we had to take the plunge, so to speak, and go on home.

As the front bumper of our car entered the moving current above the bridge, I looked out my window and read a sign I'd seen a thousand times before: ***High Water Warning! When flooded, turn around. Don't drown!*** My heart stopped but Lester didn't. The front tires hit the bridge and we started across. But, at the halfway point, the rising water lifted our two-ton car and moved it toward the other side of the small overpass.

The children and I began to scream. Lester struggled mightily with the steering wheel, pounding on the brake pedal, and whispering under his breath, "Help me God!" God helped. The driver side tires hit the low bridge railing and the car stopped moving just long enough for something to float up under the back tire and give us enough traction to move forward. If I never believed in miracles before, I certainly did on that day.

We were so blessed to have escaped. Still, we had no one to blame but ourselves. Okay, we could blame only *me*. It was I who had been so insistent we leave the house. I ignored the news about the flooded streets. I ignored the policeman who tried to warn us not to go home. I even ignored my own instincts. I was so intent on doing things my way I put the lives of my family in danger.

I am not alone when it comes to ignoring the warning signs God sends our way. In the days of the prophet Joel, the Hebrews also ignored some not-so-subtle warnings. God's people had turned away from Him. They were going through the motions but not *truly* worshiping Him. They didn't appreciate His blessings. They didn't listen for His voice or bend to His will. So, God withdrew His blessings, and as a result, bad things began to happen.

The rains the people desperately needed to fortify their fields stopped falling. Locusts devoured their crops. The sacrifices they offered the Lord were turned away. Animals they depended on for food died. Then other nations began to invade their land. They swarmed over the countryside destroying, defiling and dehumanizing God's people. Only after the destruction was complete did the people realize they had no one to blame but themselves.

Yet, God forgives, and He gave the people one more chance. Through Joel, He told them how to repent and move forward (Joel 2:12). He rescued the people from their inequities *and* from the results of their sins. The people repented and the Lord restored their blessings.

Have you just been going through the motions? Is the Lord sending warning messages your way? Is He trying to give you a second chance? If that's the case, He may be sending warning messages into your life—troubles, concerns, woes, worries, stresses and messes— because He wants you to fix what's wrong between you and Him. He wants you to turn to Him and remember He is God.

### *PRAYING TOGETHER*

*Oh, Father, creator of all that is good and holy, we pray today with purpose and with passion deep in our hearts. We love you, Lord! We beg you to send down upon us a rain of wisdom. Remind us you are God and you are in your Holy Temple. We confess our sin of neglect and ask for your*

*forgiveness. We pray in the name of your Holy Son,*
*Jesus, amen.*

### *JOURNALING YOUR THOUGHTS*

God deserves our full attention and our heart-felt worship. Ignoring him and His counsel harms no one but our selves. Use one or more of the prompts below to gauge your relationship with the Almighty. Is it vibrant and healthy? Or, are there warning signs you could be in trouble?

Look at your life today. Are you stressed? In a mess? Have your blessings been few and far between? Is God trying to tell you something? Journal your thoughts.

# Amos

Amos was a man of God, a prophet who lived during the time of Hosea, Isaiah and Micah. He, too, condemned the corruption, paganism and injustice of the northern kingdom of Israel though he, himself, was from Judah. He warned the people about the coming wrath of God, punishment for their sins. Amos encouraged them to follow God's straight path to righteousness. They did not listen. The book ends dismally. However, Amos does offer a vision of God's future pardon for generations not yet realized.

# The Plumb Line

*⁸Behold, I am setting a plumb line in the midst of My people Israel; I will not pass by them anymore.*
*—Amos 7:8*

When I was about ten, my grandfather took me with him to visit one of his friends, Mr. Baker, who was building a storage shed in his backyard. My Grandpa sat down in a lawn chair nearby chewing on the end of an unlit cigar. Grandpa teased Mr. Baker about "doing the job all wrong" and Mr. Baker teased back, saying Grandpa was a "lazy *looky-loo*". They were having a great time, but I was bored stiff. I sat in the grass nearby and pouted. Mr. Baker took pity on me and asked if I'd be willing to help build his new shed. I jumped at the chance.

He was getting ready to raise the walls of his new building and said he needed me to help him decide where to place the walls so they would be perfectly square with the floor and one another. At one corner, where Mr. Baker wanted the first two walls to connect, he held one end of a long blue string against the floor. He said to me, "Now, you go down there, at the other end, where that pencil marking is, and grab hold of the string. Hold it very tight, press it to the floor on the mark." Then he spoke to my grandfather, "Jimmy, get up out of that chair and come snap this string."

I did as instructed and Grandpa came and took hold of the blue string in its middle, pulled it away from the floor, and let it go, snapping it against the wood of the floor. A straight blue line appeared under the string. What I thought was an ordinary *blue* string was actually a *white* string dipped in blue chalk—a plumb line.

With my grandfather's help, Mr. Baker put up the first wall. The plumb line mark against the floor told them exactly where to place it so it would be square with the floor and the other three walls to come. The three of us followed the same procedure three more times. When the walls were up and the roof was attached, Mr. Baker and Grandpa pronounced the building "square."

The process of using string and chalk may seem archaic in our world of lasers and electronic levels…and that's because it is. The plumb line has been around for centuries. The plumb line is even mentioned in scripture. In Amos 7, the prophet tells about a conversation he has with the Lord in which God foretells the destruction of the Northern Kingdom of Israel.

In his vision, Amos sees locusts stripping the land of its crops. The people starve and all is lost. Amos also sees a fire—one that will, *"dry up the great deep and devour the land."*

He prays mightily on behalf of the people, and God consents to delay the apocalypse—but only for a little while.

Then God shows Amos another vision and in this revelation, Amos observes God *"standing by a wall that had been built true to plumb"* [perfectly square]. God held the plumb line in His hand. Then the Lord said,

*"Look, I am setting a plumb line among my people Israel; I will spare them no longer."*

Since the beginning of time, God has had a path laid out for his people—a straight line to follow toward righteousness. And since that time, people have wandered off the path. Being the kind and compassionate Father He is, God is willing to give His people another chance, and another *and another*, to follow the plumb line—the straight and narrow.

Although it's easy to be distracted by exciting new ideas and to be tempted by those things that aren't quite "square" with God's Word, we have to stay focused and on His plumb line. As you walk through your life this week, remember to keep your eyes on God's kingdom and your place in it!

### PRAYING TOGETHER

*Jehovah-Nissi, the Lord our Banner, we bow our knees yet raise our eyes to you this day in praise and worship. We ask, Father, that you go before us, leading us on the path of righteousness. Help us to keep our sights set on your Banner. Keep us focused and alert. Give us a passion and an excitement for living in Your Word. Remind us daily this life will soon pass away and the next, in your Presence, is our prize! We pray, Lord, with a heartfelt anticipation you will hear and answer; in the name of your Holy Son, Jesus Christ, Amen!*

### JOURNALING YOUR THOUGHTS

How do we walk through life in this secular world and not fall off the tightrope that is the road to righteousness? We can use these three simple tools to keep us steady: God's Word, prayer and trust. Use one or more of the prompts below to help you start your day on the right road and keep to the narrow path!

Which scripture speaks to the problems you are facing today?

For Example:

**Anger**—Pro 14:17, 29

**Fear**—Isaiah 43:1-2

**Impatience**—Psalm 37:7

**Insecurity**—Romans 8:31-32

**Jealousy**—James 3:14-16

**Pain**—Mark 14:36

**Suffering**—Psalm 41:3

**Temptation**—James 1:12

**Weakness**—Isaiah 40:31

Find the scripture that speaks to you and
meditate on it all day. How will it help you to
follow the straight path God has laid before you?
Record your thoughts in your journal.

# Obadiah

Obadiah, the prophet, foresaw the coming annihilation of Israel. He also knew, in advance, the part his own people, the Edomites, would play in her destruction. Edom would not only stand by and watch as Israel fell; they would actively participate in the plundering of her capitol city, Jerusalem.

Obadiah attempts, in this missive, to warn his people away from their evil plan. However, they did not heed his warnings and in time fell themselves to marauding invaders.

# To Gloat or not to Gloat

*¹²You should not look down on your brother in the day of his misfortune, nor rejoice over the people of Judah in the day of their destruction, nor boast so much in the day of their trouble.*
*—Obadiah 1:12*

Can I be honest with you? I've never really enjoyed reading the books of the prophets. For the most part, I don't really understand them. The symbolism and allegory is often over my head. I'm not stupid, just unimaginative. I guess. However, there is very little to confuse in the book of Obadiah. It's a very straightforward account of the prophet's vision and his warning to his people—Do this thing you have planned and you will suffer the consequences.

In order to really understand this prophecy, you'll need to know a little about Obadiah's people, the Edomites. They were the descendents of Esau, the oldest of twin sons born to Isaac (son of Abraham) and Rebekah. As they grew it became very apparent to all, these two boys were very different. The younger of the two, Jacob, was quiet and introverted, good to his parents and faithful to the God of his grandfather, Abraham. Esau was brutish, uncaring, un-accepting of rules and traditions. He was a real cave-man type, a man's man. Around the age of fifteen these two boys clashed. Esau ran his brother Jacob off the family estate and sent him running for his life.

Esau went another way. After Jacob left, Esau took over the family business; married two different Canaanite women (of whom his parents disapproved) and eventually turned away from the faith of his fathers. He went instead with the beliefs of his father's older, illegitimate brother Ishmael. Esau's descendents were many, and eventually became known as the Edomites.

The Edomites settled just south of the Dead Sea and built prosperous mountain fortresses in and around the Seir Mountains. They made their fortune from agriculture and cattle, and they made enemies forcing travelers to pay for the privilege of crossing their lands. Their territory put them at a crossroads between the trading nations of Egypt, Syria and Mesopotamia. All goods, thoughts and ideas, new technology, and forward-thinking advancements came through Edom.

Because their kingdom was situated high in the mountains, they were not easily defeated in war. They came to feel like they were "untouchable." They were haughty and prideful, petty and unmerciful. When the Israelites were crushed by Babylon, their land destroyed and their children and wives taken as slaves, the Edomite people watched from their mountain fortress and laughed. As soon as it was safe for them to venture into Jerusalem, they sacked what was left of the city and plundered what was left of her resources.

Obadiah predicted Edom would come "crashing down" (verse 4). Her every treasure found and looted (verse 6). He promised her allies would all become her enemies—plotting her destruction (verse 7). And, by the time it was all over, not one soul would survive in Edom (verse 8). God promised, through Obadiah, "all your evil deeds will fall back on your heads" (verse 15). And so they did.

The ruins of Petra, near the modern metropolis of Jordan, are all that is left of the Edomite kingdom. Only tourists now walk the paths where Edomite women gathered to gossip and children laughed and played. The fields where Edomite cattle grazed and crops grew in abundance are now fallow, dusty desert plains.

Although some time passed before Obadiah's prophecy came to pass, the descendents of Esau faded from history and memory. No trace of their civilization or their people can be found today. God's Word to the Edomites certainly spoke volumes: "all your evil deeds will fall back on your head."

Perhaps Paul said it best in Galatians 6:7: "A man reaps what he sows."

The smallest book in the Old Testament tells a sordid tale of hatred, cold heartedness, betrayal and retribution. It's a message extremely relevant for today. Although it may be natural—even human—to feel glee when our enemies feel pain, God expects better of us. We must be careful not to let ourselves fall into the trap of conceit or haughtiness lest our own evil deeds fall back on our heads. If you are in a position to feel glee at an enemy's pain… show grace and mercy instead. For this is what God shows to us.

### PRAYING TOGETHER
*Compassionate and merciful God, I give thanks for the opportunities you have and will place before me in which I can practice compassion and empathy—even for my enemies. I ask you to lead me away from the desires I may experience to gloat at misfortune of others, or assume those hardships were deserved. Remind me often I am blessed just to*

*be counted as one of yours. I pray these things in
the name of your Son, my Returning Savior. Amen.*

### JOURNALING YOUR THOUGHTS

In your journal, using one or all of the
prompts below, record your thoughts and feelings
about today's message: have compassion, even for
your enemies.

Is there someone in your life whom you
could call an enemy? Write a prayer for this person
in your journal. It is very hard to hate someone
you're praying for; refer back to this prayer as often
as you need to, until your heart is softened toward
this person.

# Jonah

God commissioned the prophet, Jonah, to deliver a
message to the people of Nineveh—the capitol city
of the Assyrian nation—the enemies of Israel.
Because God loves all people, Jews and Gentiles
alike, He wanted them to turn from their wicked
ways and turn to Him instead. Jonah rebelled
against God, refusing to deliver His message. He
ran away from God and was subsequently punished
for his stubbornness.

# A Whale of a Tale

*[17]The LORD provided a great fish to swallow Jonah
and Jonah was inside the fish three days and three
nights. —Jonah 1:17*

For me, one of the most challenging aspects
of being a Christian believer has been the
occasional confrontation with unbelieving skeptics.
And, it has been my experience that one of the most

common areas of doubt for the unbeliever is the story of Jonah. I can certainly understand why.

Living in northern Israel during the eighth century, Jonah was commissioned by God to bring a message of warning to the people of Nineveh, *"...for their great wickedness is come before me"* (Jonah 1:2).

Although he despised the people of Nineveh (non-Jewish pagans), Jonah didn't want to be the bearer of bad news—*plus*, he was afraid of what the people would do to him when he delivered God's message:

*"Forty days from now, Nineveh will be destroyed!"*
—Jonah 3:4

And, truth be told, Jonah believed those in Nineveh deserved God's judgment.

So, he ran. Jonah ran from God—as if he could—and went toward the land of Tarshish, in the opposite direction of Nineveh. On the way, he boarded a ship at Joppa with the intention of sailing away from God. He didn't get very far.

Once the vessel was out to sea God brought up a storm, buffeting and pummeling the ship, threatening the lives of all on board. Jonah explained to the crew it was his God causing the storm angry with him for his rebellion. The prophet suggested to the crew they throw him overboard to save their own lives. At first they resisted but faced with certain death they finally tossed him over the railing and watched him sink. The storm immediately subsided.

God did not allow Jonah to drown. Instead he was swallowed by "a great fish" (often assumed to be a whale) and there he stayed for three days and three nights.

In the belly of the whale, Jonah realized the folly of his plan to run away from the omnipotent God and repented. God forgave the stubborn man and forced the great fish to spit him out onto land.

Jonah then went on to Nineveh, delivered God's message, and saved the people. The story doesn't end there, but it is this part of the tale— *about the whale*—that brings the skeptics to my door, every time. They are always armed with scientific "facts" and "data" they believe disputes the validity of the tale.

They tell me there has never been a creature large enough to swallow a man whole. They tell me even the largest of the whales, the Baleens, could never swallow a human being in one piece. And even if there was a fish in the sea large enough to accomplish the feat, there is no way a human could survive such an encounter. Or, so say the skeptics.

As a young woman I found it hard to argue. Not because I had so little faith in the Bible, the story, or in God; but because I have always been the world's worst debater. I fluster easily, I am quickly frustrated, and I tend to become snappy and sarcastic when pushed. These things are quickly seized upon by skeptics. In no time, these types of conversations always ended with me in tears. I used to feel like such a failure, always disappointed in my inability to PROVE Jonah's story.

Since then, I've learned simpler and easier techniques for debating with Biblical skeptics. I simply say, "I cannot prove it. But, I don't need to. I simply have to believe."

It's not so hard to imagine Jonah being swallowed by a fish, staying in its belly for three days, and living to tell the tale. Not when you consider I also believe a simple carpenter was the Son of God. I believe He died on a cross, was buried in a tomb where His body lay for three days before He rose again, walked among His believers, and then ascended into Heaven—*as* God—to sit at the right hand *of* God. It may be a whale of tale but I believe. Do you?

### *PRAYING TOGETHER*

*Oh, Lord, how I worship you for being God—He who makes all things possible! You created the heavens and the earth from nothing but your Word. You have parted seas and placed rainbows in the sky. You raised Jesus from the tomb and gave Him life. For you, nothing is improbable or undoable. If you had chosen the belly of a minnow for the place of Jonah's contemplation, it would have come to pass. I believe in you and your amazing power. You are my God. I pray with the blessings of your name. Amen.*

### *JOURNALING YOUR THOUGHTS*

Many believe God no longer performs miracles, in our modern world. Do you believe that to be true? Today, write in your journal about the miracles of God in your life.

What do you believe? List your reasons for trusting (or not trusting) the literal translation of God's Word.

Can you tell a true story about a miracle in your life (or the life of someone you know) only God could have performed? Write about it in your journal.

# Micah

Micah's messages were meant for the residents of both the Northern and Southern kingdoms of Israel. He warned them their wicked ways would bring punishment from God. Yet, he tempered his warnings with good news:
One is coming who will save the world!

# The Bread of Life

*2 "But you, Bethlehem Ephrathah, though you are small among the clans of Judah, out of you will come for me one who will be ruler over Israel, whose origins are from of old, from ancient times."—Micah 5:2*

When my mother-in-law passed away in May 2003, I was asked to write the eulogy for her memorial service. I was humbled and honored to do so. However, I felt the memories and feelings shared during the celebration of her life should come from her children, those who knew her and loved her best.

So, the night before the services, I sat at the coffee table in mom's crowded little living room and asked each of her four kids to tell me something about their mother they'd never forget. As they told story after story their eyes sometimes filled with tears and sometimes joy. I began taking notes and for the first time, of what would be *many* times over the next few days, wished Mom and I had been a little closer.

Toward the end of the evening I asked them, "What one thing—a good thing—will you remember most?" Almost as one, they all said "Mom's bread." I couldn't help but notice each of them, in a very subtle manner, lifted their noses as if they could smell her fresh-baked bread. My husband said, "There was a time when she made fresh bread almost daily and with four kids in the house, we went through it quickly. The house always smelled so good!"

For my husband and his siblings, recollections of warm homemade bread bring back sweet and loving memories of their mother and better times. They're not alone. I think most of us are transported "home" when we smell fresh baked bread. I know I am. It symbolizes warmth, comfort, and most of all love.

It's not really that strange, then, when Jesus compares himself to bread.

*35 Then Jesus declared, "I am the bread of life. Whoever comes to me will never go hungry, and whoever believes in me will never be thirsty."*
*—John 6:35*

*51"I am the living bread that came down from heaven. Whoever eats this bread will live forever. This bread is my flesh, which I will give for the life of the world." —John 6:5*

*26 'And, as they were eating, Jesus took bread, blessed and broke it, and gave it to the disciples and said, "Take, eat; this is my body."'*
*—Matthew 26:26*

Even before He was born, Jesus had a connection to bread.

Let's look at today's scripture (Micah 5:2).
Many hundreds of years before His birth, Micah
had a vision about the coming Savior. He wrote:

*"But you, Bethlehem Ephrathah, though you are*
*small among the clans of Judah, out of you will*
*come for me one who will be ruler over Israel,*
*whose origins are from of old, from ancient times."*

In the original Hebrew, the word **Bethlehem**
means "house of bread." Long before Jesus ever
came in the flesh, it was foretold the Son of God
would nourish the souls of man!

It is our joy and blessing to be fed by Him.
We have to consume his teachings as if our very
lives depend upon it—because they do! Like
homemade bread straight from the oven, the Word
of God is fresh every day. It sustains us, like manna
falling fresh from heaven. It warms our hearts and it
takes us home.

If you are not in the Word on a regular basis,
may I encourage you to start? Just as our bodies
need nourishment from food and water, our hearts

and souls need to be refreshed daily by the Word of God. Consume His living bread and be filled!

### PRAYING TOGETHER

*Holy Father, I adore Thee! You are the sustainer of my soul and my joy! I pray, you will remind me each day to insatiably feed upon Your Word, to fill myself with the attributes of your character and your Spirit. Feed me with Your Word! I pray in the name of Jesus. Amen.*

### JOURNALING YOUR THOUGHTS

Use some, or all of the prompts below, to write in your journal about your efforts toward maintaining a daily walk with God.

If you do study daily, you could write in your journal about a time when God's Word spoke directly to you on a subject or issue you were facing and how it helped.

If you don't study regularly, is there a time you can remember when being able to apply scripture to your life would have been a great blessing? If so, write about it.

# Nahum

God's justice for wrong doing is at the center of this book's message. Although our God is a loving Father to His children, He must occasionally rebuke and punish them for misdeeds. This is the message delivered by the prophet Nahum.

---

# "Daddy, you're Mean!"

*²The Lord avenges and is furious. . .. ⁷The Lord is good, . . . and He knows those who trust in Him.*
*—Nahum 1:2& 7*

When my son, Jonathan, was six or seven years old, I found him playing with a box of matches. I very quickly took them away. I should have thrown them away. Instead, I lectured then tossed them onto the kitchen counter and went into another room.

Although he'd been warned not to touch them again, he did.

As soon as I left, he took the matches from the counter and when he was certain no one had seen him, ran to his room and began to light them one by one. From down the hall in the living room, I smelled that distinctive just-struck sulfur smell and came running. I caught him in the act, again! After snatching the matches out of his hand and yelling until my throat was raw, I gave him a good hard spanking.

As he lay on his bed afterwards, he cried out, "I don't like you, Mama! You're a bad mommy! You spanked me!" He didn't realize then that I was a good mother precisely *because* I spanked him!

God, too, is a good parent. When His children cross a line He's specifically told them not to cross, He punishes them for their mistakes so they'll learn not to make those same mistakes again. This is the mark of a good parent!

However, God is often accused by some of being harsh, uncaring, or just plain mean when He doles out punishment. Some people can't imagine a God who can sometimes become angry with His children. Instead, they want to imagine Him always smiling, full of goodness and light, allowing His children to do what they please, all the time.

Personally I'd have a hard time believing in a God who would allow us to skip through life that way, without consequence. For my personal relationship with God to succeed, I must view Him as my Father, my Abba—my Daddy. I couldn't do that if I knew He would allow me to get away with things harmful to me and others. My physical father would never do that!

Take the people of Nineveh. In the time of Nahum, the Ninevites were a cruel, vicious, and wicked people. They worshiped pagan gods, made sacrifices of the innocent, and brutalized the people in surrounding nations

God had had enough. He sent Nahum to bring a warning of destruction and obliteration to the Ninevites. Like Sodom and Gomorrah before her, Nineveh had fallen so far into corruption, she could not be saved again (recall the book of Jonah).

Although the Lord is patient and loving, He will not allow the wicked to continue in their sport without punishment. He will seek justice. When He does, God's retribution is always righteous.

I remember all those years ago, when I spanked Jonathan for playing with matches, it hurt my heart to make him cry. However, I would have done it again in a heartbeat if I'd found him putting himself in danger again. It's the job of parents to protect, guide, and rebuke their children on occasion. We give our children boundaries and we expect them to live within those limits for a reason. It's the same with God. If we, as His children, could just learn to live within the confines of His loving arms, we'd be so much better off.

Are you living within God's limits? If not, maybe it's time to ask yourself why not. Drop to your knees and ask Him to forgive you of your sin, and ask Him to teach you within His Will. God is a forgiving and oh-so-loving God. He's reaching out for you with open arms. Take the leap and reach for Him, too!

### PRAYING TOGETHER

*Abba, Father, how comforting it is to know you are willing to correct me when I stray from the boundaries and limits you have set for me. Lord, I ask you to always be there, guiding me, loving me, punishing me when you must—so I may grow—*

*because you are a good parent, a loving Father. I*
*pray these things with love, Amen.*

### JOURNALING YOUR THOUGTHS

It's time to share your thoughts with your
journal!

Choose one of the following statements and
write your opinion about your choice in your
journal:

(1) I believe God's punishments to be cruel
and unwarranted.

(2) I believe God's punishment are just,
righteous and necessary.

# Habakkuk

Have you ever seen God? Habakkuk did, but only after he complained to God about His decision to punish the people of Israel with the hammer of Babylon. Habakkuk thought it was unfair to use such a sinful people to bring about Jerusalem's downfall. Although God had no reason to justify Himself to any man, He chose to give Habakkuk a unique insight into His plan.

# Reaching for the Light

*[19]The Lord God is my strength; He will make my feet like deer's feet, and He will make me walk on my high hills. —Habakkuk 3:19*

When my family and I first moved to Las Vegas, we were pleasantly surprised to discover there was so much more to do here than visit "The Strip." Don't get me wrong. That famous run of casinos and hotels is beautiful and fascinating. However, when you live here, it's nice to know there is more to do than gamble—especially when you're not a gambler.

After we settled into our home, one of the first places we visited was the Red Rock Canyon National Conservation Area. The mountains there are just gorgeous.

As nature freaks and rock-hounds, my husband and kids tumbled out of the car and started climbing those big red rocks before I even had my seatbelt unhooked!

Although I love the outdoors like my family, my health normally prevents me from taking on mountainside opponents. I have Rheumatoid Arthritis and more-often-than-not suffer from crippling joint pain. Knowing I would not be hiking, I grabbed a book to read as I got out of the car and waved cheerily at the backs of my goat-like clan as they ran off toward adventure. I sat down in the nearest clump of grass I could find and began to read.

I was asleep with my chin on my chest and my book pages fluttering in the wind when my husband and son showed up beside me a little while later and said, "You've got to see this!" They dragged, pushed and sometimes carried me up the mountain between them. The climb terrified me. Yet, the view from the top was worth every moment of dread. What a spectacular world God has given us to live in—*rent free*!

The vista spread before me was one of the most beautiful sights I have ever seen. Although the red rocks of the Canyon are somewhat barren of large trees, all around us scrub brush and tumbleweeds competed for our attention with cactus and flowering shrubs. Greens, yellows, magentas, and blues softly and sweetly colored the landscape. My heart almost stopped. How glorious is our God!

In addition to the beauty on the ground, there was a large cloud formation hanging in the sky. Coming from the center of one of those cottony billows and bursting through like a sword was a single shaft of sunlight. Although the day was bright and sunny, that one shaft of light seemed somehow brighter, more concentrated, and shinier than all the light around it. Like a pointing finger, it highlighted the land right below it. Just off-center of the beam stood one single Joshua Tree (or Yucca Palm).

Joshua Trees grow in abundance in the desert. In some areas they are so closely cropped together they appear to be one giant plant instead of many. Yet, this particular Joshua Tree stood by itself with nothing around it for several hundred feet but grass. One of its branches stretched out from the top. It appeared to be reaching for that shaft of sunlight.

In my imagination, I pictured human desperation, a frantic desire to be a part of the brightness, touched by the light. I sat down there on the top of the mountain with my imagination stirring and feelings of awesome wonder filling my head and heart.

I thought of a passage I once read in the book of Habakkuk,

*"The Lord God is my strength; He will make my feet like deer's feet, and He will make me walk on my high hills." –Habakkuk 3:19*

My passage up the mountain was anything but deer-like. I was neither swift nor sure. If my husband and son had not been on either side of me I would never have reached the pinnacle—or even tried. But with their help and strength, I was able to see God's glory at its fullest from there. Habakkuk tells us it is like that in the kingdom of God. We can only reach the heights of His splendor with His help. Without it, we're like the Joshua Tree; stuck in one place, striving for and almost touching glory, but unable to reach the light.

Whatever it is you're trying to do without Him today…stop! Let God be your strength. Let Him carry you to the top of the mountain. Take it from me. The view from there is amazing!

### *PRAYING TOGETHER*

*Heavenly Father, how amazed I am at the work of your hand! I praise and worship you for being the Only God of Creation! Thank you, Lord, for taking me to the high places and revealing to me your glory. Thank you also, Father, even for the valleys. For if I had never experienced the low places, if I did not know the darkness, I would not recognize how incredible the light from the mountaintop really is. I pray in the name of your Son, Jesus, amen.*

### *JOURNALING YOUR THOUGHTS*

Are you facing a seemingly impossible task, a mountain of stress, fear, doubt or anxiety? There is no reason to dread! God can carry you up and over any mountain you face. Spend some time writing in your journal, about the rocky climbs you're facing and the strategies you can employ to reach the top!

What keeps you from charging that mountain and overcoming that situation?

Circle One: I will   or   will not   give my problem to God, today, and ask him to carry me to the top of the mountain. Why did you choose the answer you did?

# Zephaniah

The people of Judah had become arrogant and ignorant. They worshipped idols and sacrificed their brothers to appease created gods. The prophet Zephaniah gave them messages from the Lord warning of His judgment. King Josiah took to heart Zephaniah's words and put into place sweeping reforms banning human sacrifice and the worship of man-made gods. Unfortunately, it was too little too late.

# I'll call you

*³ Seek the LORD, all you humble of the land, you who do what he commands. Seek righteousness, seek humility; perhaps you will be sheltered on the day of the LORD's anger. —Zephaniah 2:3*

I can be neglectful of God. Can't you? There are days when my head gets so wrapped up in the bills I have to pay and the errands I need to run, I forget to pray. There are times when my grandkids and their antics are more entertaining to me than what I could learn from my Bible, and there are times when I'd rather stay at home in front of the TV than go to church.

Is Zephaniah talking to me? Is he talking to you? You bet he is. Not because we miss an occasional worship service, but because we don't put God first in our lives all the time! If we don't change our ways, if we don't renew our daily worship of and love for the one true God, then we could suffer the consequences. We could separate ourselves from His love.

Imagine this: You're in a room full of happy, joyous, smiling people. In their midst is Jesus. He is warm, loving, caring, and adoring of all those He can see and hear and touch. You're at the edge of the crowd, blocked by the multitude. You can see Him but can't reach Him. You jump up and down, calling His name, but he doesn't seem to hear you. Your heart aches to feel His touch and yet, you can't get through. Finally, he looks your way and says, "I'll call you" and then …walks away.

"*I'll call you?*" At first you're insulted and a little bit angry. How dare He ignore you? And then it hits you. You remember all the times you did the same to Him. "I'll pray later, Lord." "I'll go to church next week." "I'll study Your Word right after my favorite show." This is what *I* imagine hell to be like… God treating me the way I've treated Him.

However, there is good news. Zephaniah's book ends in joy. Zephaniah tells the people that God's purification will bring them back to the Father. They will be restored. They will be glad and rejoice in Him. They will no longer need to fear or mourn because,

*"The Lord your God is in your midst, the Mighty One, will save; He will rejoice over you with gladness, He will quiet you with His love, He will rejoice over you with singing." —Zephaniah 3:17*

I dream of a day when He will rejoice over **me** with singing. I tremble with anticipation when I imagine His attention pouring over me like perfume. I long for the time when He will quiet me with His love, *in person.*

We can't let the idols of our time (TV, Facebook, money, ambition, etc.) keep us from the

Lord. He deserves our attention, adoration, and worship. Put Him first and He will rejoice over you with gladness!

### PRAYING TOGETHER

*Dearest Lord, God of my fathers, I pray that you will redeem me from my mistakes. I pray you will forgive my neglect and my shameful treatment of you. Remind me every day to put you first; to run to you first; to think of you first. Help me O Lord to be worthy of you; I pray these things in the name of Jesus, our Returning Savior, amen.*

### JOURNALING YOUR THOUGHTS

In your journal today describe how it would feel if Jesus treated you the way you treat him.

# Haggai

Haggai's prophecy was directed to Zerubbabel, the governor of the restored Israelite community, and the high priest of the Temple, Jeshua. The book of Haggai includes five prophetic messages meant to encourage the speedy restoration of the Temple with underlying warnings discouraging rebellion against God.

# Mea Culpa! Mea Culpa!

*$^{10}$Therefore, because of you the heavens have withheld their dew and the earth its crops.*
*—Haggai 1:10*

I once read an article about a kidnapper who sued his victims because they didn't do enough to help him evade the police as the authorities closed in for his arrest. The same article told about a particular law student who, after failing the bar exam (several times), sued his law school for failing to educate him adequately. There is also the case of the burglar who sued the owners of the home he burgled because their dog bit him as he entered their residence, illegally. *Really?!*

Unfortunately, yes…really. These insanely frivolous lawsuits are but the tip of today's iceberg. Sadly, we have become a nation of blame-slingers. We blame our bosses because we don't make enough money. We blame our spouses for our own unhappiness. We blame the government. We blame the economy. We blame our neighbors, family, and friends. We blame everyone—even God—without ever pointing the finger in our own direction.

It's not our fault we're obese—we'll blame the fast food industry. It's not our fault our kids misbehave—let's blame the schools. It's not our fault we overspend—it's the fault of TV advertisers for making us want the things they sell.

None of us is blameless! Even if we were, that righteousness would not protect us from bad things happening in our lives. Look at Job of the Bible. See what happened to him? He lost everything from his cattle to his children in a very short time. Yet, he was blameless in God's eyes. Are you blameless? I know I'm not.

The truth is, sometimes—*whether we are good people or not*—bad things are going to happen. Moreover, there will be times when what happens to us *is* actually our fault. We will make choices that will alter our lives in ways that bring us pain. We will zig when we should have zagged. We will say yes when we should have said no. We do wrong when we could have done right. These things will cause chaos in our lives.

The Book of Haggai clearly states, it is "because of you [God's people]" the land dried up. The people chose wrongly. Their choices resulted in God removing His blessings from them. And, just like the people of Israel, there will be times when our choices will result in God removing His blessings from us. However, the Bible tells us to be humble, to pray, and to turn to Him to see our fortunes restored *(2 Chronicles 7:14)*.

If things are upside-down in your world right now, if you're in pain, if you're suffering because of decisions you've made, there is a way to ease your burden; talk to God. Humble yourself to the Lord and ask forgiveness for sin separating you from Him. Allow your heart to bear witness to your faith in Him. Let Him bring about change. God will restore you. Not because you deserve it, but because He is merciful. Be aware, however, it might not happen overnight. God's timing is not our timing. But God *is* in the business of blessing. Your turn will come!

### PRAYING TOGETHER

*Mea Culpa! Mea Culpa! Mea Maxima Culpa! Father, it is my fault, my most grievous fault there is sometimes a wall between you and me. I build that wall, brick by brick, when I make decisions which go against Your Will. Thank You, Lord, for I know I've been forgiven, even before I stop writing because you are the God of love. I pray in the name of Jesus, your most precious sacrifice, given on my behalf, amen.*

### JOURNALING YOUR THOUGHTS

We bring so many of our problems upon ourselves, yet, so many of us blame God, instead. Some feel He has neglected them, at best, or is punishing them, at worst. What do you think?

Think about your current situation. If things are tense or problematic in your life, who would *you* say is to blame?

Can you see a future in which you can look back on your current problems and thank God you experienced them?

Why or why not?

# Zechariah

Zechariah the prophet was sent by God to the recently released captives of Babylon to encourage and sustain them as they rebuilt the Temple of Solomon.

# When You Can't, He Can!

*⁶So he said to me, "This is the word of the LORD to Zerubbabel: 'Not by might nor by power, but by my Spirit,' says the LORD Almighty.*
*—Zechariah 4:*

I hadn't slept all night. I'd tossed and turned and worried until I was both physically ill and heartsick. Concerns over un-payable bills, my kids, and health issues kept my mind running in circles all night. I climbed out of bed more exhausted than I'd been the night before, when I'd crawled into it and I dreaded the day to come.

As I trudged into my office, half asleep and completely distracted, I tripped over a pile of toys left on the floor by my grandkids. Hopping around on one foot, cradling the other in my hands, biting back a squeal and a few choice words, I landed in my desk chair with a thud, banging my knee on the handle of one of the desk drawers. Tears came to my eyes as I mentally cursed every toy manufacturer on earth.

After much hissing and whining, I opened my planner and glanced at all the things I had scheduled to accomplish that day. For a moment, I saw spots before my eyes. The list was staggering: laundry, dusting, bathing the dog, filing our taxes, cleaning off my desk, making a casserole for a sick friend, Bible study, a dreaded phone call, a doctor's visit, and more. My brain rebelled! *"Are you serious?"* I asked myself out loud. "I can't do it. I just can't do it." I threw myself back, hung my arms over the sides of my chair in defeat, and began to cry in earnest.

From our bedroom, my husband heard me howling and got out of bed to check on me. Wordlessly, I handed him my list. He read it as he gently patted my back and then said, "The dog is a dog. She can go one day without a bath—maybe even two or three. Have Lizzie (our granddaughter) do the dusting. The taxes can wait until next week—or later–it's only January. We can buy a bucket of chicken for Melly (our sick friend). And laundry can wait until tomorrow or the next day. That cuts your list by more than half. As for the rest," he turned to leave the office, tapping his finger on my Bible which was sitting on my desk as he walked by, "…first things first." Then he went back to bed. My husband is a very wise man. He says the right thing and then leaves before I can argue.

Zechariah, too, was a wise man and a prophet of God who brought hope to the people of Israel when it was in short supply. The people were faced with the almost insurmountable task of rebuilding the temple. For nearly seventy years, Solomon's temple had lain in ruins, a result of the almost complete annihilation of the Hebrew nation by the Babylonians. Once free from captivity, the Israelites vowed to raise their temple to its former glory, but they were not without opposition.

Fearing the political and religious strength of a renewed Israel, the Samaritans and other neighboring nations vigorously worked to hinder, harass, and halt the Israelites in their endeavor. Petty scheming, vandalism, and even violence against the builders finally put a temporary halt to the reconstruction. The people lost heart in the face of what seemed like impossible odds. For two years the newly rebuilt foundation lay abandoned, awaiting new construction, and then came Zechariah with a message of hope and optimism.

His prophetic vision gave buoyancy to the dreams of the people. Their expectations of what *could be*, with the help of God, grew wings. Through Zechariah, the people were given a message from God—you can't, but I can! Their hearts were renewed along with their determination and strength. Soon Solomon's temple was standing again.

We, too, can find hope in Zechariah's message. We don't have to be powerful. We don't have to be mighty. We don't even have to get through our list of chores each day—not on our own. God is our strength. Lean upon the Lord today. It's the only way.

### PRAYING TOGETHER

*Lord, you are God and we praise your name in heaven and on earth. Bear us up when we can no longer stand. Encourage our hearts and build our determination to give the best that is in us to you and your Holy Kingdom. We pray in the name of the Highest, Jesus, our Returning Savior, amen.*

### JOURNALING YOUR THOUGHTS

Today, while journaling let your minds roam free. Answer honestly and genuinely. Reflect upon your answers and decide how they may impact your life.

Who do you turn to in times of difficulty? Make a list.

Where does God fall on that list, *honestly*? Why?

# Malachi

The prophet Malachi spoke to the people during a time when the spiritual life of the Israelite community was at an all time low. The intention of Malachi's message was to warn and encourage the priests and the people.

---

# The End of the Rainbow

*[10] "Oh, that one of you would shut the temple doors, so that you would not light useless fires on my altar! I am not pleased with you," says the LORD Almighty, "and I will accept no offering from your hands. —Malachi 1:10 (**KJV**)*

At twelve years old, I became a Rainbow Girl. The Order of the Rainbow Girls is a world-wide Christ-centered organization designed to give young girls the tools, training, and encouragement to become leaders in their communities.

By the time I was fifteen, I had risen through the ranks to become the "Worthy Advisor" of Fort Worth Assembly #15. My job was to preside over meetings, plan and supervise activities, and act as hostess at social events (with the help of adult sponsors—of course). I was so proud of my position and title! It didn't take long for me to discover I loved being the girl other girls admired.

When I was fifteen and had been Worthy Advisor for about three months, the Rainbow Girls hosted a car wash. Although there were adults at the event, I acted as if I were solely in charge. Unfortunately, I was not doing a very good job.

Within the first thirty minutes, some of the girls and I were spraying each other with the hoses, dumping buckets of water over each other's heads, throwing sponges filled with soap, chasing one another, and generally acting like silly little girls. Although we had a line of cars waiting to be washed, we were just too busy playing to care.

We were having such a good time I did not notice my good friend, Carrie, sitting on the sidelines, looking upset. When I asked if she was okay, she responded by saying, "I'm so mad at you I could just slap you!"

I was shocked! What did I do? When I asked, she yelled at me, "You sprayed me with water and got my hair all wet! I have a date this afternoon. I worked all morning to look nice and now, thanks to you, I look like a drowned rat!"

I tried apologizing but she didn't listen. The longer she ranted and raved, the angrier I got. Finally, I let loose all the irate words building up in me.

I said things—*and used words*—I never should have, but I didn't care. Then, I turned around and saw our adult advisors standing right behind me. I was in big trouble. Pat, a family friend and my sponsor, pulled me aside and chewed me out (deservedly so).

She made a point of reminding me that as the Worthy Advisor of our group, it was my responsibility to keep the girls on track. We weren't there to have fun. We were there to raise money for a charity. "How many people do you think we can feed with the money you've raised so far? Not many, I can tell you that," she said.

Then, she *really* socked it to me. She got onto me, as only a mother-figure could, about the language I'd used and about responsibility, leadership, appreciation for the position I'd been given, and lady-like behavior (or the lack there-of). She outlined just how miserably I'd failed in every category.

Being a leader is one of the hardest things anyone can do. When others are looking to you, you should be looking to the Lord. This is exactly the message God delivered to the priests in Israel through Malachi around 500 B.C.

Just like me, they had allowed their position of leadership to go to their heads. They became lazy, offering defiled and unworthy sacrifices. They stopped honoring God and were instead, honoring themselves. As a result, God removed his blessings from the priests *and* the people. He would not, could not, accept their sacrifices. Doom and destruction followed.

As employers and employees, mothers and wives, church leaders and Christians, we have to be aware we are always being watched. Our actions reflect on those we lead. We have to ask ourselves (often), are we leading them in the right direction? Or, are we like the priests of Israel, leading them to destruction?

## *PRAYING TOGETHER*

*Lord in heaven, we honor you and praise your name. We want so much to please you; to bring you sacrifices that will honor you and bring you glory. As we are the example for others, be our example. We pray in the name of Jesus, amen.*

## *JOURNALING YOUR THOUGHTS*

Everyone follows someone or something. The question is, who is following you and where are you leading them?

Make a list of all the people who might be following you. (For example: your children, co-workers, classmates, neighbors, employees, friends, etc).

Are you surprised by the length of the list?

Finish this sentence: Looking forward, I now realize as an example to others, I must…

# Matthew

The first of the four Gospels, tradition tells us that Matthew's version is a record of the Savior's life through the eyes of one of His first disciples. Written by a Jew for a Jewish audience, Matthew's book begins with the Savior's ancestry, tells of His many miracles and teachings and ends with His death on the cross and His subsequent glorious resurrection.

# Mountaintop Experiences

*[1] After six days Jesus took with him Peter, James and John the brother of James, and led them up a high mountain by themselves. [2] There he was transfigured before them. His face shone like the sun, and his clothes became as white as the light.*
*—Matthew 17:1-2*

There are some people in my life that I love to listen to. Their voices and turn of phrase are just mesmerizing. However, there are others who aren't quite as eloquent. For example, there was once a woman in my life who described just about every experience in *her* life as "a mountaintop experience".

o "I had my nails done at this wonderful new place. It was truly **a mountaintop experience!**"

o "I had the most exhilarating **mountaintop experience** in Macy's the other day…"

o "The last episode of *Desperate Housewives* was just a heavenly **mountaintop experience** for me! Wasn't it the same for you?!"

Uh…no…

So, what *are* mountaintop experiences, anyway?

Mountaintop experiences are those moments with Jesus that make us go "AHA!" or "OH!" or "AAAAH…" They are the times in our lives that break, soften, or quicken our hearts.

These moments are life changers. They are often described as those times when—amid the chaos and clamor of regular ordinary life—God shows us He is with us. They tell us God is God and all is right with the world.

Let's look at one famous mountaintop experience told of in Matthew chapter 17. This is the story of Jesus' transfiguration. (It can also be found in Luke and Mark.) Most everyday Bible readers like you and I have no real clue what this story is all about, and even some theologians admit to being as stumped as we are.

We have questions. I do, anyway. For instance: why did Jesus climb to the top of the mountain to meet with Elijah and Moses? Why these two men? Why not Abraham and Methuselah, or Adam and David? What did they talk about? What news did they bring necessitating a personal visit from heaven? And why did they leave so quickly once the conversation was over?

Moreover, it's not just the participants of the conversation that leave me wondering. I also have questions about what happened *while* they were talking. The Bible tells us the Savior's' *"...face shone like the sun, and his clothes became white as light."* What is that all about? Was God there on the mountaintop, too, taking part in the conversation, but invisible to the witnesses? Was it

His presence that made Jesus' face glow? Probably, but no one seems to know for sure.

What we do know is Jesus and his disciples were changed by this experience... In that moment, Peter, James and John saw Jesus as he actually *was*. For the first time they realized He was more than a mere man. They knew, without a doubt, He actually was the Son of God. It wasn't just a theory they were working with or a belief they held in their hearts. It was a truth they gleaned from God Himself; they heard God's voice! *"This is my Son, whom I love. Listen to Him!"*

From that moment on, they knew all they'd ever need to know. They had just been witness to and taken part in an "AAAAAH!" moment—a ***true*** mountaintop experience.

Have you ever had a moment like this with Jesus? Have you experienced Him in a way so vivid and real, so spiritual and awakening, so life changing and exciting it changed your life? Communicate that story with others! Even though Jesus asked His disciples to keep this particular incident to themselves—until His full glory could be revealed—it should be your joy to share your mountaintop experiences with others, today! It's just too good to keep to yourself!

### PRAYING TOGETHER

*Father God, I praise you and worship you for being the one true God. The God who changes lives and brings glory and amazement to ordinary moments. I pray when others look at me they see the remnants of my mountaintop experiences with you! I pray in the name of Jesus, the Light of the world. Amen.*

### JOURNALING YOUR THOUGHTS

Some life experiences, though not easily defined or communicated, can be life-changing. They can shape opinions, ideals and futures. Share with your journal today about a time when you may have experienced a moment such as this.

Describe a time in your life when you may have experienced a life-changing or life-shaping moment with Jesus.

Did the experience alter or shape your future in any way? If so, how?

# Mark

Tradition tells us this Gospel was written by John Mark, the friend and traveling companion of Paul, and the "spiritual son" of Peter. The events recounted here by Mark are believed to be Peter's eyewitness accounts of the ministry of Jesus. The book focuses mainly on His last week on earth and is written to persuade a Gentile audience into a belief in the Christ.

# All You Need Is Love

*[16] And he took the children in his arms placed his hands on them and blessed them.*
*—Mark 10:16*

I have four beautiful grandsons. All four are amazing little boys. They're also rambunctious, rough, rowdy and loud—*very* loud.

The favorite pastime of the two older boys is to play "fight," a game in which they pretend to punch, kick, and karate chop each other and the invisible "bad guys" while yelling "POW!" "BAM!" and "WHACK!"

They also love to play "sojers." Like most little boys, they have hundreds upon hundreds of little green army men. They'll sit for hours setting them up just to knock them down again. Then, filling their little hands with the little green men, they throw them around the room screaming— "BOOM!" "BANG!" "KA-BLUE-Y!" It's all very thunderous and piercing to the eardrums.

Just like the rest of us, however, all four occasionally get very quiet and want to be held and loved on. They want assurances they are wanted and adored. They want to hear whispers in their ears of all the wonderful things we feel about them. They want to feel safe and valued.

Long ago, the followers of Jesus brought their little children to Jesus to be blessed by Him. He took them into his arms in just this way. He hugged them tightly and whispered in their ears the things they needed to hear. He told them they were wonderful. He told them they were beautiful. He told them they were smart, and kind, and *special*.

He made them laugh and feel warm and protected. He made them feel cherished.

However, when the disciples saw Jesus cavorting with the children, they tried to shoo the children away. There are more important things to do today than play, they said. Yet, Jesus rebuked them. Why? Because he knew, better than anyone, love is all we need.

Occasionally we need to climb into the lap of God like little children—*with wondering eyes, open hearts and minds like sponges.* We need His assurances. We need to know He loves, values and rejoices in us.

We can memorize the Bible word for word; we can go to church every day of the week and twice on Sundays; we can throw ourselves into charitable work and be good examples to everyone we meet…but if we can't love God and allow ourselves to be loved in return… *What. Is. The. Point?*

I once had a very similar conversation with a young teen that had just recently begun to think about becoming a Christian. I was telling her how much I needed Jesus' love to get me through some days. I mentioned how stressful my life was, and how if I hadn't been able to take Jesus with me wherever I went, I would have been lost. She said, "Oh yeah. Like Mary!"

*Huh?* Which Mary? Did she mean Mary, the mother of Jesus? Mary Magdalene? Mary, Queen of Scots? How did any of them fit into the conversation we'd been having? She began to recite a poem I'd heard many times before and suddenly I understood.

"Mary had a little lamb, whose fleece was white as snow. And everywhere that Mary went, the lamb was sure to go..."

Without even realizing it, my new friend had completely summed up my point simply and succinctly. Jesus is the lamb white as snow. If we keep his love in our hearts all day, our spirits will always laugh and play.

### *PRAYING TOGETHER*

*Father God, Abba, Daddy, how wonderful it is to be able to run into your arms and know I am safe. I can come to you in times of sadness and joy and you will hold me close and make me feel loved. I love* **you** *and praise you and thank you, God, for the gift of your Son, Jesus, amen.*

### *JOURNALING YOUR THOUGHTS*

Do you carry the love of God with you everywhere you go? Do you run to Him when you need encouragement? Let your thoughts flow freely concerning today's reading.

When I am with Jesus I am most often more like *the disciples* or *the children* in our scripture reading today. Choose one. Explain

# Luke

Not one of the original twelve disciples of Jesus, Luke was instead a Gentile physician who became a believer and traveled with the Apostle Paul spreading the Gospel. According to tradition, Luke recorded the story of Jesus for a Greek speaking audience of Gentiles focusing upon Christ's humanity while still glorifying the deity of the Savior.

# Trust and Obey

*¹As Jesus looked up, he saw the rich putting their gifts into the temple treasury. ² He also saw a poor widow put in two very small copper coins. ³ "Truly I tell you," he said, "this poor widow has put in more than all the others. ⁴ All these people gave their gifts out of their wealth; but she out of her poverty put in all she had to live on." —Luke 21:1-4*

Mike was a wonderful Sunday school teacher. My husband and I loved attending his class for young marrieds under 30. His lessons were fun, informative, and spiritually motivating. I can't tell you how many times Lester and I left church so jazzed with what we had learned from him we went right out and tried to put each lesson into practice.

For example, one Sunday Mike explained how important it was for Christians to give from the heart, not their surplus. He read from the passage above, (Luke 21:1-4).

At that time in our lives, Lester and I were very much like the widow of the story; we had no surplus. We were surviving on peanut butter and jelly sandwiches for breakfast, lunch and dinner. Mike's lesson spoke to us in a very fundamental way. Because of our situation we had not been tithing. In fact, we never had. We were waiting for that moment, *sometime in future*, when we could give from our surplus.

That Sunday in class, Mike asked us this question, "***Do you trust God or not?*** Do you trust Him to take care of your needs? Do you believe your God is big enough to handle your situation—big enough to feed you, clothe you, love you and bless you, big enough to cover you in miracles—even if you put your last two pennies in the plate.

Or, do you instead think of him as being too small and too weak to cover your needs.

Lester and I realized we had been putting God in a very small box. We had not trusted Him with our money. We trusted Him with our souls…but not with our grocery money, not with our rent, not with our last two pennies. Mike said, "How can you truly trust the Lord with your eternity if you can't trust him with your wallet?"

We practically ran home that Sunday afternoon to turn over couch cushions, and look under beds and in cookie jars to find every last penny we could, to give to God. The deacons were probably surprised the next week to find rolls of pennies in their offering plates.

Lester and I haven't always trusted enough to give from our hearts. But let me tell you, it was the times when we did, when we weren't afraid; when we trusted and believed in Him, and gave all we could—though it wasn't always very much— that everything turned around for us. When there was no food in the pantry, friends dropped by and invited us to dinner; Lester was offered overtime he hadn't been expecting; relatives sent money and the electric company extended their due date! God will not let you down. Trust in Him and be blessed! Give from your heart; He always does.

### PRAYING TOGETHER

*Thank You, Heavenly Father, for your blessings and bounty! I praise you and sing your name with glad tidings. You are a generous God. Help me to be trusting and believe in you; to give from my heart and not just my surplus. Help me to remember your eye is on the Sparrow. How much more so, on me! You will provide! I need only to believe. I pray in the name of Jesus the Christ, amen.*

### JOURNALING YOUR THOUGHTS

Today I have only one question I'd like you to ask yourself; journal honestly and completely about your feelings and thoughts on this issue. Come back in six weeks and see if anything has changed.

Do I trust God, or not?

# John

The apostle John, the best friend of Jesus, focused his Gospel on Jesus' miracles and spiritual teachings. Some stories found in his book are not found in the other gospels. For example, the story of the raising of Lazarus from the dead is found only in John's version. His mission was to help others realize Jesus was more than a human being, to emphasize the Savior's deity and oneness with the Father and Holy Spirit.

# Step Out of the Boat

*[16] When evening came, his disciples went down to the lake, [17] where they got into a boat and set off across the lake for Capernaum. By now it was dark, and Jesus had not yet joined them. [18] A strong wind was blowing and the waters grew rough. [19] When they had rowed about three or four miles, they saw Jesus approaching the boat, walking on the water; and they were frightened.*

*—John 6:16-19*

Do you have faith… in your faith?

Do you ever wonder just how strongly your beliefs would hold in the face of opposition? Temptation? Persecution? Do you ever ask yourself—do I really believe everything I've been told? Do you wonder if your faith is strong enough to hold you up on water?

If so, you're not the first to question your faith. Even the disciples, who walked with Jesus, talked with Jesus, lived, laughed and learned from Jesus—in the flesh—had the occasional faith failure.

There was a time when Jesus sent his disciples across the Sea of Galilee in a boat, by themselves. Essentially he said, "I will meet you later." The disciples assumed, as anyone would, that Jesus would catch a ride on another boat or take a day or two to walk around the Sea of Galilee (which is really just a great big lake) and meet them on the other side.

However, when they were far out in the middle of the water, they heard Jesus calling to them as he strode across the surface of the sea. Most of the disciples fell to the floor of the boat, curled themselves into the fetal position, and began to whimper. They were terrified. They believed they were seeing a ghost. Peter, however, stood at the railing and called out to Jesus, "Give me faith to walk on the water and meet you halfway." Jesus said, "Come."

Peter stepped over the edge of the boat, full of faith and took several steps on the glassy surface of the sea before he looked down, became frightened, lost faith and began to sink.

Some people criticize Peter for his lack of certainty. Even Jesus said, "Ye of little faith." He asked, "Why did you doubt?"

In my own humble opinion, Peter doesn't deserve flak for sinking—at least not from the likes of us. Peter is the only one of twelve disciples who stepped over the edge of the boat! The others cowered inside the boat crying like babies. Peter was the only one not afraid of the Lord. He was the only one willing to try and experience walking on water. Sure, it only lasted a few steps…but he did it! Peter is my hero!

If you're facing your own "walking on water" dilemma, don't be afraid to doubt. Everyone has doubt.

Sarah doubted—and became the mother of nations. Jacob doubted—and fathered the twelve tribes. Moses doubted—and still led the people to the Promised Land. Even Jesus doubted and had fear:

*"Going a little farther, he fell with his face to the ground and prayed, 'My Father, if it is possible, may this cup be taken from me. Yet not as I will, but as you will.'" —Matthew 26:39*

AND, YES! Peter doubted—but, he *did* walk on water…even if it was just a step or two.

It isn't doubt or even fear that condemns us. It is the failure to face that doubt; the failure to believe in a God who will carry us through that makes us cowards. When we feel we aren't good enough and worry about failure, or when we believe we can't do it alone, we're being human. However, if we allow it, God strengthens us, keeps us strong, and moves through us to succeed where we fail!

Have faith in the Lord Almighty! Step out of the boat!

### PRAYING TOGETHER

*Father God how amazing you are! How you thrill my heart! Even when I doubt and fear, you are there to strengthen me and to move me forward in your will. Father, I thank you for having patience with me even when I let my feet get wet… I pray these things in the name of He who said," Yet, not my will be done but yours." Amen.*

### JOURNALING YOUR THOUGHTS

Are you experiencing a fear of the water? Do you worry about stepping out of the boat and sinking? You *should* worry if you don't have God in your life. Today, I would ask you to write in your journal about your fears and your strategies for overcoming them.

What am I afraid of? (For example: Going back to school, seeking a new job, getting a divorce, singing a solo during services, becoming a parent, leading a ministry…). Write about your worst fear.

Ask yourself: Do I trust God to strengthen me and help me to push past my fears? Why or why not?

# Acts

Tradition tells us the book of Acts was written by Luke and is a continuation of the story he began in his letter to his friend, Theophilus (in the book of Luke). It focuses on the story of the beginning of the church, on the Apostles who were its foundation, and the believers who carried it further. Luke describes how the Holy Spirit—God's representative on earth—empowers His people to share His good news and spread the message that GOD LIVES!

# "In the Beginning..."

*⁸But you will receive power when the Holy Spirit comes on you; and you will be my witnesses in Jerusalem, and in all Judea and Samaria, and to the ends of the earth. –Acts 1:8*

"Anyone can write. Fourth graders across America are writing book reports about Tom Sawyer. Businessmen are writing interoffice memos and email. Housewives are writing recipes and letters to their mothers. **Angst-ridden teenaged girls are writing dark, depressing, and badly written poetry because this boy or that one has disappointed them in some way. Anyone can write…but, it takes talent and creativity to be an author. You have neither, but I will teach you."**

And that's how my semester with Professor "X" began.

My first writing assignment, **"write a MYSTERY that will interest me"**, didn't. **"Boring first sentence; were I not paid to endure this kind of drivel, I would not have,"** came the feedback.

My second assignment did not fare much better: **"Write a LOVE STORY that will affect me so much I'll want to buy roses for my wife after reading it."** Since I'd gone to school with his wife and loved her dearly, I really wanted to see to it that she got roses. As with the first assignment, the critique of my second work was less than encouraging. **"I was not moved to bring my wife roses after reading this claptrap. In fact, so**

**disenchanted was I by this nonsense, I slept in
the guestroom after reading it."**

So it went assignment after assignment
until… **"Write a story that will change my life."**
By this time in the semester, I had lost all hope of
impressing that man. I was just doing the time to get
the required credit. So, when it came to this latest
assignment, I asked myself, what could I possibly
write that would change *his* life? With a shrug and a
devil-may-care attitude, I set about writing
something, *anything*, to fill the required four pages.
It was like free association on steroids.

I began with this all-important first
sentence:

*"In the beginning was the Word, and the Word was
with God, and the Word was God."*
*—John 1:1*

I wrote about my faith, my belief in the one
true God and Jesus Christ, His Son. I wrote about
how both had changed *my* life. Truthfully, at that
point I didn't care if I changed *his* life or not. I just

wanted to get through the class with some shred of my self confidence still intact.

When I collected my graded paper from the professor a few days later, it looked as I had anticipated it would, so covered in red marks and stinging criticism I thought my eyes would bleed. Yet on the last page, in handwritten print almost too small to read, my professor had written:

**"You need much more work and experience before you can ever call yourself an author. But don't lose hope. Although, this piece did not change my life (After all, I am Jewish and let's face it, it wasn't all that well written), I did find it intriguing. Good use of a first sentence. It 'grabbed' me. But I would not recommend plagiarizing the work of other writers in the future."**

In the years that followed, with God's help and blessing, I *have* actually changed the lives of others with that same story. Although I'm not sure my writing skills have improved all that much, I have honed and enhanced the method with which I deliver God's Good News. I am not Billy Graham. In fact, I would call my evangelizing style more of an accidental happenstance each time it occurs. But, I am impassioned by my love of God and His work in my life. And, I'm willing to share the story and change lives. Are you?

### PRAYING TOGETHER

*Father, how inspiring you are! Your message and your promises are so intriguing they forever change the lives of those who hear and believe! I am proud to be your daughter and prouder still to share your Word with those who would listen. I am yours. I pray, Father, with the promise you will hear. I pray in the name of Your Precious Son, Amen.*

### JOURNALING YOUR THOUGHTS

Not everyone is cut out to be a TV evangelist. Yet, Jesus did charge us _all_ with spreading the gospel.

*"With my authority, take this message of repentance to all the nations…"— Luke 24: 47-48 (**NLT**)*

In your journal today, write about your role as a witness to Jesus' glory

Being willing to share my faith does not necessarily require me to stand on street corners and evangelize. How then might I share the gospel instead?

Is my life a living example of my faith in God?

*"Share the gospel at all times. When necessary, use words."* —St. Francis of Assisi

# Romans

While he was in Corinth during his third missionary trip, the apostle Paul began making plans to travel to Rome to assess the progress of the church there. He wrote this epistle to introduce himself and summarize the Gospel of Christ before he arrived. One of the most important messages he gave the Christians in Rome was that in Christ, we are all new creations. We no longer need to conform to this world, for there is a better one waiting!

# The New Square!

*²Do not be conformed to this world, but be transformed by the renewal of your mind, that by testing you may discern what is the will of God, what is good and acceptable and perfect.*
*—Romans 12:2 (**ESV**)*

Once when I was searching the Internet for a new fruit salad recipe, I stumbled across a webpage about square watermelons. Yes, I said square. It seems the Japanese love watermelon but don't care for its size (it's too big for their tiny refrigerators). So, they found a way to create a better mousetrap…uh, watermelon.

While baby melons are still on the vine, Japanese farmers slip the tiny fruits into square glass boxes which sit on the ground next to each vine. As the watermelon grows, it conforms itself to its transparent prison and becomes square instead of the oval shape nature intended. Although the Japanese people, as a whole, are thrilled with the *idea* of square watermelons, only the wealthy can afford this unique fruit. In order to recoup the time and resources involved in growing square watermelons, farmers must charge 10,000 yen a piece for their special fruit. That's roughly $82! Eighty-two!

A Japanese newspaper reporter interviewed an obviously wealthy grocery store patron who was purchasing twelve of the expensive square watermelons. When asked why she was willing to spend so much money, she replied, "All my friends are buying them."

Conformity can sometimes be an expensive choice.

In the book of Romans, Paul tells us we should steer clear of conforming to the secular world, its thoughts, actions and ideology. Unfortunately, not only do we sometimes rush to conform, we also do our best to help our friends conform, as well! It seems no one wants to be different. We read the same questionable books and watch the same dubious TV shows. We wear the same fashions, say the same things; we practically live the same lives.

However, according to Paul, fitting in is exactly what we should try to avoid. Doing what others are doing, saying what they're saying, and thinking like they think is a trap. Not only will we risk our morality and standards by trying to become part of the crowd, we will also risk our uniqueness.

God gave us our individuality while we were still in the womb. This is a beautiful truth. He made us who we are for a purpose! We are God's exclusive creations, and we are worth so much more than the ordinary.

Define who you are in God, with God, and through God. Break away from the crowd and be different! Don't be a square. Be a Christian!

## *PRAYING TOGETHER*

*Gracious God, Master Gardener, you have created each of us to be unique and beautiful and special in your eyes. Teach us to be grateful for being special and set apart. We are extraordinary and blessed to be loved by you! I pray in the name of Jesus, Amen.*

## *JOURNALING YOUR THOUGHTS*

Although it is sometimes hard to take a stand and be the one person outside the circle of conformity, it is often the right thing to do. Write in your journal today about your struggles (*or lack thereof*) to stay separate and unique.

Write about a time when you set yourself apart from others.

# 1 Corinthians

Corinth was a Greek city in which Paul established a Christian church during his second missionary journey. Unfortunately, after Paul moved on, the church quickly disintegrated. Believers lost touch with the Good News, and began questioning Paul's authority. Worse, they began to question the deity of Jesus and whether or not he really rose from the dead. Paul's epistle was his attempt to set things right again.

# Sticks and Stones

*[4]My conscience is clear, but that does not make me innocent. It is the Lord who judges me.*
*—1 Corinthians 4:4*

Have you ever been the subject of taunting, bullying, teasing, rumors or criticism? Chances are very good you can say yes to at least one of these— especially if you ever attended high school. Kids can be cruel little beings. Sadly, some never grow out of it. Adults, too, often act barbarically toward one another.

Although we've been taught "Sticks and stones can break our bones but words can never hurt us" ...the truth is, words *do* hurt. Hateful words, cruel taunts, vile lies and deceitful rumors can often cause more painful scarring and more horrible trauma than any broken bone.

The apostle Paul knew this better than anyone. Some members of the church in Corinth, a church *he* seeded and helped to grow, allowed themselves to be deceived into believing some pretty awful lies about him—*and Jesus*.

False teachers in Corinth led some in the church to believe Jesus had been *just* a prophet. They taught Jesus was *not* the Son of God, had *not* risen from the dead, and had *not* ascended into heaven. They acknowledged his good character and the importance of his message. Yet, denounced his deity.

Moreover, these false teachers led many members of the Corinthian church to accuse Paul of not being a true apostle. They said he had no authority to preach or teach in the first place. They claimed Paul had imagined his meeting with the resurrected Christ on the road to Damascus or had made the whole story up to give himself credentials he had not legitimately earned. They accused him, too, of stealing money from them and other churches in the form of housing, food, and wine.

Not only did many in the Corinthian church turn against Paul, they shared these lies with others, and rumors spread like wildfire. When these stories reached Paul in Ephesus, he was heartbroken—and outraged.

It is from this pain and concern for the church itself, the epistle we call 1 Corinthians was written. In it Paul defends the deity of Jesus and he defends himself as if he were on trial. In his letter, he counters every false claim with truth. He said,

*"I care very little if I am judged by you or by any human court; indeed, I do not even judge myself. My conscience is clear, but that does not make me innocent. It is the Lord who judges me."*
*—1 Corinthians 4:3-4*

Although ugly words *do* hurt and malicious lies about us can be damaging, we need to remember as Paul did; only God's opinion of us truly matters in the end. If you're facing personal persecution, try to remain strong. Keep your eyes only on what is good and true and beautiful—God! He loves you so.

### PRAYING TOGETHER

*Father in heaven, Abba, I come to you today on behalf of my brothers and sisters who may be hurting, stung by the words or actions of others. I pray you will rain down on them your tears of compassion and cooling mercy. I pray you will strengthen them and give them the courage to face each new day with true confidence in you. Let them feel your power as they face those moments of pain. Fortify them with the knowledge only you can judge them with authority. All others, wolves howling in the wind, are nothing more than noise. I pray with the authority of Jesus, who said, "ask and it shall be given", amen.*

### *JOURNALING YOUR THOUGHTS*

Are you in pain because of the words or actions of others? Spend some time today journaling about your experiences.

Describe a time in your life when you were hurt by lies, rumors, hateful words or the actions of others.

Did you rely on the love of God during this time of your life? Why or why not?

Does the knowledge that only God's opinion of you truly matters help you now?

# 2 Corinthians

The people of Corinth had injured Paul deeply. It hurt him when they doubted the deity of Jesus and questioned his own authority to teach. When they continued their slander against him, even after his first letter, it broke his heart. 2 Corinthians was Paul's second attempt to reconcile with the people of Corinth and bring the church back together again.

# Forgive and Forget

*18All this is from God, who reconciled us to himself through Christ and gave us the ministry of reconciliation... —2 Corinthians 5:18*

Eighty-four-year-old Alice Jane Biggs is anything *but* big. In fact, weighing only ninety pounds and standing barely five feet tall, Alice is quite delicate and tiny. Yet, the powerhouse personality of this woman makes her seem anything but small. By the sheer force of her presence she takes command of any room she enters and becomes the center of attention, and the star of the show.

Because of her joyous, infectious laugh and her sincere, rib-cracking hugs, she also makes friends quite easily. However, as warm and inviting as Alice can be when she is happy, she is just as cold and intimidating when she is not. There's one person who particularly brings out this infrequently dark side—her sister, Claudia.

Like her older sibling, seventy-nine-year-old Claudia is also tiny and delicate. She, too, is boisterous and charming. She has dozens of loyal friends and admirers and she, too, is loving and cordial to everyone…except her sister.

These two ladies, once close and loving best friends, are now the bitterest of enemies. Their feud causes a tension in the family that is palpable and consuming. Cousins avoid cousins, nieces and nephews avoid their aunts, and no one mentions the other faction—all in the name of keeping the peace. It's shameful and hurtful for all involved.

What would keep a loving Christian family in such a state of upheaval? A serving dish—of all things—a serving dish!

Many Christmases ago during a family brunch at Claudia's house, Alice and Claudia began what seemed like a friendly debate over the origin of a particular serving dish in Claudia's cabinet. Alice said the dish had once belonged to their maternal grandmother. Claudia contended the dish had instead belonged to a great-aunt. The debate went on through brunch and into dessert. What had begun as an honest difference of opinion in the morning had become a major battle by late afternoon. Voices were raised, harsh things were said and, in a moment of pure frustration, Claudia picked up the dish and slammed it onto the floor shattering it into millions of tiny pieces.

"There! Now it doesn't matter who it belonged to before me. Does it?"

For several moments, Alice stood in her sister's kitchen surrounded by stunned family members, her mouth agape and her fists clenched. Then, without a word, she turned on her heel and left. The two women haven't spoken since.

There was a time when human beings separated themselves from God just as Alice and

Claudia separated themselves from one another. The people turned from God's living water and began to partake in sin and wrongdoing. Their iniquity built a wall between them and God. Every lie, murder, adulterous activity, pagan worship—*every sin*—placed another brick in the wall. The Father was heartbroken by the separation. He loved and missed His children. So, sacrificing His whole being as only a Father could, God surrendered His only Son to break down the wall and reconcile His people to Himself. WE are those people!

What He asks of us in return is simple—that we do as He did, and take on the ministry of reconciliation…to forgive and forget.

Forgiving others is one the hardest things we can do. Most of us avoid it as long as we can. What we fail to realize is NOT forgiving others only causes **us** more pain—it's an exercise in futility. Holding on to anger and hate in a misguided attempt to make a point or hurt the other person serves only to separate us from a full relationship with the Lord.

Think about this: God forgave you.

Is there someone in your life you need to forgive?

### *PRAYING TOGETHER*

*Father of love, creator of harmony, I come to you today with a heavy heart. It is time to forgive the one who hurt me. I ask, Father, you help me to find in my heart a desire to forgive—to let go of the hurt. Help me to get over the past and learn to live in the here and now! I believe I can do all things through your Son who strengthens me. Amen.*

### *JOURNALING YOUR THOUGHTS*

Every message has a point. Every journey has an end. The point of this message is for you to end your struggle with unforgiveness.

Don't wait for an apology from the other person. You may deserve one, but if you're waiting for one, you may be waiting a long time. God can't wait. He didn't wait for <u>your</u> apology before sacrificing His Son, *for you*! Write a letter or call the other person and share your forgiveness; or, write about it in your journal. Even if you're not ready to speak to the other person, forgive them *today*!

# Galatians

In this epistle to the church at Galatia, Paul defends his belief that Christians are not obligated to follow Mosaic Law (Jewish tenets given to Moses by God). Paul reminds his readers of Abraham's place in history—as the father of the Hebrew people— and beloved by the Lord long before Moses was ever born. Abraham was accepted by God simply through an act of faith. In this same way we, as Christians, are established in God's kingdom by faith and faith alone.

## *Sola Fide—Faith Alone*

*³"Are you so foolish? After beginning by means of the Spirit, are you now trying to finish by means of the flesh?" —Galatians 3:3*

My relationship with Julie began when she and her sister visited a Bible study I was leading. Although she was quick to say she'd been "dragged kicking and screaming" and didn't believe in "Christian nonsense," we tried to make her feel welcomed and comfortable. I even lent her my Bible so she could follow along as we read scripture. At first, she didn't bother to open it. As we went along, however, she seemed to become genuinely interested in the topic and began taking notes. Before long, she had my Bible open and was asking questions and making comments.

At the end of the evening she asked for my phone number, which I gladly gave. Over the next few weeks we talked together on the phone several times as I gently nudged her spirit toward the Lord. It wasn't easy. She was incredibly resistant. She'd been raised to believe in many types of gods and many different viewpoints. For example, she was an avid believer in Tarot cards and astrology.

I was fighting an uphill battle.

At one point, I nearly gave up. I felt my inexperience in such matters was somehow hindering her decision. I asked my pastor for advice. His answer was simple: "Keep at it." So I kept at it and sure enough, with her sister's help, Julie eventually accepted Christ as her Lord and Savior.

Months passed. In that time, Julie never missed a Sunday worship service or a Bible study class. She became a member of the choir and volunteered in the nursery on Wednesday nights. She often cooked for the men's group and went to every ladies fellowship meeting. She volunteered almost every week to bring the desserts, or make the craft, or be the one who called to check on those who could not make it. Everyone was incredibly impressed by her dedication.

Then, after nearly six months as a Christian, Julie dropped out of sight. She stopped attending church. She quit the women's fellowship group; she stopped volunteering, and didn't attend Bible study classes. After a few weeks, I called, and she invited me to her home so we could talk.

She finally shared with me her reasons for being absent for so long. She explained how hard it had been to keep up with her work schedule, her grand-children's school and sport programs, *and* church. "I know I won't get into heaven unless I do those things at church, but I'm just so tired."

Flabbergasted, I asked where she had gotten the idea she had to *work* to get into heaven. I never told her that! She explained, "A girl at work, another Christian, told me I had to do 'good works' for God to love me." It took the rest of the day to convince her she did not have to earn her way into heaven.

None of us could ever get to heaven on our own, no matter how hard we work! Our humanity, our very DNA condemns us as criminals—*from birth*—as sinners in the flesh. We could never do enough good works to erase every sin. Thank God we don't have to! We have hope in the Lord's mercy and grace and His willingness to welcome us home through faith alone.

The Bible says:

*"For God so loved the world that he gave his one and only Son, that whoever believes in him shall not perish but have eternal life."*
*—John 3:16*

What a beautiful promise. It tells us all we have to do is believe!

In Latin, this concept is called Sola Fide or "faith alone." Because God is a loving God, He made a way for us through the sacrifice of His Son. Jesus' death on the cross erased our criminal records and left us blameless before God. The only "work" we're asked to do in order to gain entrance into heaven is to believe Jesus was the Son of God. We must believe He died on the cross for our sins, and rose again to ascend into heaven.

God does compel us to care for our fellow human beings. We are asked to feed the hungry and clothe the naked. We're asked to lead the blind and care for the sick. We are asked to be merciful and kind and loving to all. Yet, mercy from us is not *required* like a ticket at the gate of heaven. He only asks us to give what He Himself has freely given.

### PRAYING TOGETHER

*Dear Christ Jesus, how my heart sings your praises! I am blessed beyond measure by your mercy and grace. Never could I buy my way into your presence; never could I earn my entrance into heaven. Yet, I know I will meet you there in the clouds someday, solely because I believe. I stand on faith alone. I thank you God, for that's all I need. I pray in the name of my Savior, Jesus, amen.*

### *JOURNALING YOUR THOUGHTS*

Using the prompt below spend some time today journaling your thoughts about faith and your life in Christ.

Write about the moment you realized you had faith in Christ Jesus.

Was it sudden? Did it happen all at once? Did someone lead you, or did you find Him on your own? Were you frightened, thrilled, excited, or moved?

# Ephesians

Paul's purpose for writing this book was to encourage new believers during a time of persecution. In this epistle, he defined God's presence from before time began, through the present age, and into the future. He also deals with practical matters of Christian relationships like marriage.

# Only the Strong Survive!

*[21]Submit to one another, out of reverence for Christ.*
*–Ephesians 5:2*

My husband and I have been married for more than thirty-five years.

On occasion we have been asked, "What's the secret to your long marriage?" Our answer is almost always the same, God *and tenacity*.

Marriage isn't easy. It takes patience, compromise, mutual respect, and love; plus, a pigheaded and rigidly unbending aversion to giving up or giving in.

That's the message I've always wanted to pass on to my kids: You can't give up.

Before my son married in September 2009, I thought my husband and I should sit down with him and give him tips, pointers, and ideas for a happy marriage. I said as much to my husband who replied, "Oh no you don't! He has to figure it out for himself, just like the rest of us. Marriage is a test of manhood and only the strong survive!"

He was joking, of course. Yet, he's not wrong. You *do* have to be strong to make a marriage work. And, one of the strongest decisions any two people can make is to ask God to be a part of their union. Lester and I have faced so many trials and tribulations, so many disappointments and failures, tragedies and changes, it's a wonder we've gotten through it all. Conversely, we've also experienced abounding joy, triumphs aplenty, passion, excitement, and unlimited happiness. However, I don't think we could have gotten through *any* of it without God!

Have you invited God into the midst of your marriage or relationship? If not, do so today. Only the strong…with God's help…survive.

### PRAYING TOGETHER

*Father in Heaven, I pray you will move in the midst of my Christian sister's marriage or relationship. As she reads this, today, strengthen her resolve to include you in all facets of it. Open her eyes to the Words written by Paul and give her the tools to make her marriage work, despite the efforts of the enemy who may be working against it. I pray these things in your name, God Almighty, amen.*

### JOURNALING YOUR THOUGHTS

Spend some time today exploring your relationship?

Is my bond strong enough to survive without God? Why or why not?

# Philippians

While in prison, Paul wrote this letter to his friends in the church at Philippi. It is basically a thank-you letter for all they had done for him while he was with them. Paul also writes about some of the issues he was facing while imprisoned. However, despite the fact he was confronting the death penalty; he rejoiced in God and encouraged the church to do the same. He also used this epistle to chasten two female parishioners in Philippi who were disrupting church relations with their bickering.

---

# Called by Name

*[2] I plead with Euodia and I plead with Syntyche to be of the same mind in the Lord.*
*—Philippians 4:2*

I can remember a time when, as a fifth-grader, I found myself in quite a bit of trouble for talking in class. I was very excited about the field trip planned for later in the day and the very idea of being out of the school building on an adventure, and away from books and assignments, had me trembling with anticipation. I began giggling and whispering to a friend sitting in the desk next to mine.

Never turning away from the blackboard where she was writing a math problem for the class, the teacher called out, "Class, settle down. No talking." Embarrassed, I slammed my lips together, but only for moment. As soon as she began marking on the board again, I began to whisper again. Mrs. Jackson turned to face the class and again admonished *everyone* for something I alone was doing. "Class, I know you're excited about the field trip. Right now, however, we're supposed to be learning, not talking."

I was chastened enough to stop whispering, but not for long. The third time Mrs. Jackson was forced to stop teaching; she turned and looked straight at me. "Angela Beck, I'm not going to ask you again to stop talking."

I had never been so embarrassed. She called me by name! Everyone was looking at me. Several of the other girls began laughing and giggling at my expense and one of the boys called out, "Busted!" I don't think I spoke another word for the rest of the day.

I wonder if Euodia and Syntyche were as embarrassed as I had been when Paul called them by name in his letter. Although we don't know what they were bickering about it, it is apparent the story of their strife had been carried from the city of Philippi all the way to Paul, in prison, in Rome. They were probably mortified. However, the problem between these two was causing dissension in the church, and it had to be stopped.

By calling Euodia and Syntyche by name, Paul got their attention and the attention of all who read the letter. He did not criticize these two women. He did not make a list of their transgressions. He did not condemn them or reprimand them harshly. He simply asked them to have the right attitude in God:

> *"...and 'love your neighbor as yourself.'"*
> *—Matthew 19:19b*

It's simple. Scripture doesn't tell us we have to be best buddies with everyone we know. We don't even have to like everyone we know or meet. However, God does expect us to treat each other with dignity and grace. He expects us to avoid conflict, retaliation, and revenge. He expects us to turn the other cheek. He expects us to lead by example, forgive one another, and not allow disagreements to turn into strife, disrupting the church or our lives. To sum it all up, He expects us to love one another the way He loves us.

> [35] *"By this all men will know that you are my disciples, if you love one another."*
> —John 13:35

### PRAYING TOGETHER

*Dear Lord, how blessed we are to have your Word as our teacher. Train us to be silent, to listen to your voice as you guide us through each lesson and fill our hearts with love. Give us compassion for our neighbors along with patience and wisdom. We want to live as you would have us live. We pray in the name of Jesus the Christ, amen.*

### *JOURNALING YOUR THOUGHTS*

The truth is conflicts between neighbors (friends, co-workers, family members, etc.) are going to occur no matter how we try to avoid them. We are each unique individuals with differing opinions and ideals. It is our response to conflict that's important.

The last conflict I had was with _____ and was about _____. (Write the story.)

Answer the following questions about that time in your life:

Did I handle myself in a way I'm proud of today?

If I answered "no" above could I have handled things differently? If so, how?

# Colossians

While captive in Rome, Paul wrote this letter to the church at Colossae. His heart was filled with alarm concerning rumors about strange practices and theories creeping into the congregation there—Judaic ritual, astrology, mysticism, and even the practice of magic. Worse still, these same *(supposed)* Christians had demoted Jesus from the Son of God to the role of angel or simple human prophet. Paul's letter explains the deity of Christ and the power and authority he holds, not only as God's son, but *as* God.

# The Power of His Name

*[17]And whatever you do, whether in word or deed, do it all in the name of the Lord Jesus, giving thanks to God the Father through him.*
*—Colossians 3:17*

Richard Leroy Watkins was a Korean War veteran from Huntington, Indiana. He was a graduate of both Purdue and Ball State Universities, where he earned Bachelors and Masters degrees in mechanical engineering and education. Although he was brilliant, he was said to be awkward and uncomfortable in social situations, and did not make friends easily. Richard Watkins never married nor had any children. Sadly, at his death in August 2007, he was homeless, an atheist and for the most part, alone. For all the things Mr. Watkins *was* at his death, there is one thing he was not—penniless. Richard Leroy Watkins died a millionaire.

This fact was discovered upon his death, when his vast wealth was distributed to several charitable organizations. Even though during his life, Mr. Watkins had had the power to save himself from cold nights, hot days, and loneliness, he *chose* to live as if he was desperate and destitute. I can't help wondering why he would choose to live a life of apparent powerlessness.

Yet, Mr. Watkins is not alone in this decision. Without realizing it, most of us make that same choice every day—to live a life of helplessness—despite having limitless power at our fingertips. Let me explain.

Jesus once spoke the following words:

*"... All authority in heaven and on earth has been given to me."—Matthew 28:18*

In the original text, Jesus used the Greek word "exousia," which means to do as one pleases or the authority of kings (Strong's Concordance #1849). In other words, he was saying he is in control. He also said:

<sup></sup> *3 "And I will do whatever you ask in my name, so that the Father may be glorified in the Son."*
*—John 14:13*

Simply put, this means all authority in heaven and earth is at our disposal. He is king of the universe, ruler of all, and He answers our prayers. With faith there is nothing we cannot do!

Of course, there is a catch. Our wishes, wants, and desires must be in God's will, and we must be grateful and give praise to God for everything in our lives.

What this means is, I may pray for a new car with faith strong enough to move mountains, but if a new car is not in God's plan for me, I'm not going to get a new car. He might, however, provide me with a friend who can take me places, a bus ticket, or a sturdy pair of new shoes. My job is to be thankful even though my driveway remains empty. The power does not rest in my prayers, but in my God.

It is my choice—and yours—to utilize the power of His name every day. We could remain helpless and desperate trying to depend on ourselves in every situation, or we can choose to rely on God and the supremacy He has over every circumstance in our lives. It's a simple choice. For me, it's also an easy one to make. How about you?

### *PRAYING TOGETHER*

*Heavenly Father, King of the Universe I bend my knee in supplication to you. I praise you, Lord, and thank you for all the blessings in my life. I am so grateful I can come to you with my burdens, my joys, my wants and needs and in your will be satisfied! You are God and I am blessed to be counted among your faithful. I pray in the name of Jesus, amen.*

### *JOURNALING YOUR THOUGHTS*

Are you allowing your wealth in the power of God's name to sit unattended and unused while you live a life of quiet desperation?

Big or small, I call on God for help with all my problems. True or False? Write about why you answered the way you did.

I believe God knows what's best for me and answers my prayer accordingly. Why or why not? Record your views.

# 1 Thessalonians

Paul's letter to Timothy, who was living and working at the church in Thessalonica, was intended for encouragement, instruction and affirmation. The church was being persecuted, the believers were losing faith and perverting doctrine, and many were living lives unworthy of Christ.

---

# It's Okay to be "The Bad Guy"

*[14] And we urge you, brothers and sisters, warn those who are idle and disruptive, encourage the disheartened, help the weak, be patient with everyone.*

—*1 Thessalonians 5:14*

One of my favorite contemporary Christian songs in recent years is "We Are" by Kari Jobe. Every time it comes on the radio, I reach for the dial to turn it up as loud as I can. I want to hear every note and every word. As I sing along, I am always re-energized and refreshed by it: *"...we are called to spread the news, to tell the world the simple truth, Jesus came to save, there's freedom in His name..."*

I especially love the chorus, which reminds us we are the light of the world.

As Christians, it's our job to shine the light of Jesus. We are to be bright and shining examples of His love. We are to encourage one another, bolster the weak, and be patient with those who test our patience. We are to strive to unify the brotherhood, and sometimes, we are to admonish one another when we do wrong.

*Wait...what?* I didn't sign up for that! What others do or don't do is none of my concern. *Right?* Wrong.

The Bible tells us in 2 Timothy 3:16 and in our passage today (1 Thessalonians 5:14) that it *is* our duty to keep one another on the straight and narrow path. We have to help one another with Biblical teaching and correct thinking.

I have to admit to you I was one of those Christians who once said, "Oh no. Not me. Not my job." I never minded encouraging or edifying others, teaching, leading, guiding…. I could do those things. Or, at least I could *try* to do those things.

However, when it came to admonishing…well, let's just say "avoidance" was my middle name. At least it used to be. Then I found myself in a position of Christian leadership. There was no way to avoid doing my job—which sometimes included admonishing those to whom I ministered.

Yes, it's sometimes difficult and painful. Yes, it's awkward, uncomfortable, and it can be embarrassing. It's hard to tell a fellow Christian they've strayed from the path of righteousness. But *not* correcting another child of God could be more harmful to everyone involved. One awkward conversation in the here-and-now could avoid a lifetime of pain and misery for that person and others.

Perhaps you have a sister (or brother) in Christ who is making wrong choices and/or living a life not worthy of Him. Paul tells us it is our duty as Christians to help them see the light and put their feet back on the path to righteousness **gently and with love**.

Let me give you some _suggestions_ for doing this the right way.

First, pray. Then, be certain the issue before you is real—not the opinion, rumor or gossip of others. Check the facts. Be prepared to go to your loved one with only what is right and true. Secondly, pray. Ask God for his guidance and support. Be sure to listen for His answer and know in your heart you're doing the right thing. Thirdly, pray and go with compassion and love. Be gentle and kind. Don't accuse or threaten. Make no insinuations and lay no blame. Lastly, pray _together_.

I will not lie to you. This will not be easy. However, done in God's will—with His support—it may be the best thing you've ever done for someone else.

### *PRAYER JOURNAL*

*El Shaddai, You are our Heavenly Father, the one who corrects and chastens when your children do wrong. In your Word, you've charged*

*us with keeping each other accountable in this same
way. We are to admonish sin with love and
gentleness. We pray you will strengthen us and
equip us with your care and mercy. Give us the
courage to stand up against sin—no matter what the
cost. We pray these things in the name of the Son,
Jesus the Christ.*

### *JOURNALING YOUR THOUGHTS*

You may not be a member of Christian
leadership, but you are a Christian. Sometimes that
means standing up for what's right, confronting
others about their behavior and being the bad guy.

Have you ever had to confront a Christian
brother or sister about their behavior?  Write about
it.

Were you able to rewind history, would you
do it again? Why or why not?

If you answered yes above, explain what (if
anything) you would do differently.

# 2 Thessalonians

Unable to return to the city of Thessalonica, Paul sent his young protégé, Timothy, to check on the believers there. He was joyfully surprised to hear from Timothy that the church had begun to grow strong and sturdy roots in his absence. However, the believers there worried they had somehow missed the second coming of Christ. This epistle was meant to assure them this was not the case.

# The Devil Is Coming!

# The Devil Is Coming!

*³Don't let anyone deceive you in any way, for that day will not come until the rebellion occurs and the man of lawlessness is revealed the man doomed to destruction. —2 Thessalonians 2:3*

My friend, Mary, is a reasonable, intelligent, independent, and sophisticated woman. She and I are good friends and have quite a bit in common.

We like the same foods, love the same movies, and enjoy the same fashion styles. We even agree when it comes to politics. There is only one subject on which we don't see eye-to-eye—the end of the world.

In the summer of 2011, Mary and I began hearing about millions of people all over the world who had begun to set their affairs in order. They said goodbye to loved ones, quit their jobs, and blew their kid's college funds for one last "trip-of-a-lifetime" all because they didn't expect to wake up on December 22, 2012. People believed the world would stop spinning on December twenty-first because some silly cycle on some silly Mayan calendar, carved into rock centuries ago, was set to end on that day.

Let me see if I can explain. December 21, 2012 marked the last day of a 5,125-year-long cycle on the Mayan Calendar. Many assumed this last day of the cycle would be last day of the world. New Age doomsday-soothsayers predicted the earth would drop into a black hole, be hit by planet-killing asteroids or explode from the inside out on that day. Mary became one of many ardent believers in the Mayans ability to predict the end of the world.

I don't understand it. Still don't. However, what I do understand—in my life—is the power of God's Word and I can tell you *God* says the end of this world (*as we know it*) will come like a thief in the night and no man may know its schedule. No man, not even the Mayans.

Only God is control. That is exactly what Paul told the believers in his letter to the church in Thessalonica.

*[3]Don't let anyone deceive you in any way, for that day will not come until the rebellion occurs and the man of lawlessness is revealed, the man doomed to destruction.* —2 Thessalonians 2:3 (NIV)

There are several things that have to happen in this world before God chooses to end it. One of those things is the *man of lawlessness* must appear. You may have heard him called—*the antichrist*. This man will appear out of nowhere and take over the world. He'll set himself up as a humanitarian, a peacemaker and a friend to all. He will perform miracles, signs and wonders. He will be much admired and beloved by legions of followers. Leaders from all over the world will turn to him and defer to him. He will demure in false modesty as they crown him king but...he *will* sit upon the throne of power, and one day rule the world. It is then his true colors will seep through.

Under his reign greed, envy, violence and tyranny will be loosed. The one-world currency will be set in place as will the global identification system—every human being who falls to his power will be marked in some way. No one will be able to buy or sell without the mark. Non-believers of the new king will be persecuted, hunted and killed...

It isn't a pretty picture, is it? In fact, it's rather frightening. Yet, there is hope; so says the apostle Paul.

*⁸And then the lawless one will be revealed whom the Lord Jesus will overthrow with the breath of his mouth and destroy by the splendor of his coming.*
*—2 Thessalonians 2:8*

The man of lawlessness will not succeed. He will be overthrown and Jesus Christ, the True Savior, will reign on the earth forever and ever. Amen!

Neither the government nor the churches, nor any man *or Mayan* can predict the second coming of Christ. Nor can anyone predict the end of the world. It will happen, when it happens, *at God's say so*, and not a moment before. This is where Mary and I parted ways. She believed the Mayans to be in charge of time and the future, and I believe God to be in control. The question is… what do you believe?

### *PRAYING TOGETHER*

*Dear Father, how we love you. What a blessing it is to know it is YOU who is in control of the universe, the world and of our small lives. I cannot, will not worry about the future because all I have is today. I pray in the name of the Lamb, Jesus the Messiah, amen.*

## *JOURNALING YOUR THOUGHTS*

Today I just have one question for you to answer inside your journal. *What do you believe?* Using descriptive words and images describe your faith in God. Is it strong? Does it waver? Why or why not? Do you lean on it during times of trouble? Do you stand firmly on the rock of salvation? Take time today to really think about your faith. If it needs work, try to pinpoint where and how. Pray God will open your eyes to your relationship with Him and help you to make it stronger every day.

# 1 Timothy

The importance of living a righteous life is the theme of this book. It is a letter written by the Apostle Paul to his young friend, Timothy. Paul had commissioned the younger man to lead the church in Ephesus while its members struggled with issues of faith, religion, and lifestyle preferences. Paul's epistle is an encouragement to both Timothy and the church toward making right choices and good decisions.

# $^{20}/_{20}$ Vision

*⁵The goal of this command is love, which comes from a pure heart and a good conscience and a sincere faith. —1 Timothy 1:5*

A long time ago, when I was a new mother, I went through a phase my husband called my "heritage kick". I was obsessed with genealogy, antiques, keepsakes, and the like. I even developed a mania for heritage tomatoes—*just because of the name*! For me, everything old was new again.

One facet of my obsession was quilting and quilts. For weeks, I shopped for an antique quilt for my daughter's nursery. Since we were poor as church mice, I could never find one I could afford. So I chose to make one. This was a very strange decision when you consider I did not know how to quilt. Nor did I have anyone in my life who could teach me. I didn't even own a book about quilting. However, none of that was going to stop me.

I went to work. I chose my fabrics, drew my design, and started cutting out seven-inch squares with a pencil, ruler, and pair of scissors. (Every *real* quilter reading this just groaned out loud and winced in pain!) I didn't know any better. As a result, not one of my squares was actually...well, square.

When I started, I intended to cut all the blocks I'd need at once, but I was young and impatient, and couldn't wait until they were all done. So I began the hand-sewing, embroidering and quilting process with the first 12 squares I'd already cut—ambitious and stupid.

By the time I finished with those 12 blocks, I'd grown bored with the whole project. And, let's face it, it was so hard! (Who knew?)

My husband suggested I throw it all away but I just couldn't do it. It *was* a mess…but it was my mess. So I put my unfinished project away in a closet and forgot all about it.

Two years passed before I would pick it up again.

When I did, it took only a few moments to realize I was facing a pretty big hurdle. Not only could I not remember the cut dimensions of the original 12 squares, I still didn't know how to quilt! I guessed at the dimensions and began cutting new eight-inch blocks.

When I tried attaching the new blocks to the original 12, they wouldn't fit. My original blocks had been seven-inches squared and the new ones were an inch bigger. The truth is I never noticed this discrepancy. Too dumb to see it, I guess, I forced the edges together and made them fit anyway!

After nearly a year of work, I completed that quilt.

It *is* beautiful (at first glance) and my daughter, who is in her thirties, treasures it still today. However, as you can imagine, it is a very flawed creation.

It does not take an expert eye to see where I went wrong. Not only is the quilt enormous, it is also oddly shaped. The top section flares out almost a foot wider than the bottom part. All you have to do is trace the tucks and folds and stretched seams to find my mistake(s). It's a mess.

It's just as easy, for some of us, to look back with 20/20 vision and see where we've gone wrong in life. All we have to do is trace the questionable decisions, the wrong turns and bad choices. What's funny is that it's pretty easy to see where we've gone **right**, too.

Looking back into our past, we can all probably trace the right choices that led us to Jesus. I know I can. Before him, my life was a mess. After him, everything changed for me. I began making decisions with a purer heart, a good conscience, and a sincere faith. Every good thing I've ever done; every smart choice I've ever made; every moment of joy; every act of kindness and love can be traced back to that one point—the moment I invited him into my life.

Don't get me wrong. My life is flawed. There is no question about it. There have been times (and there will, most likely, be more of them) when I force my will upon God's pattern…and, it doesn't quite fit. So yes, I can look back and see the folds, tucks, and stretched seams of my own artistry marring the beauty of God's covering over my life. And yet, the overall creation is still beautiful. I can say that because He makes it so.

### PRAYING TOGETHER

*Holy Father, I am so thankful for the moment I gave my life to Jesus. He made me into a new creation, something beautiful in your eyes. I pray you will guide me in all I do toward a purer heart, a good conscience and sincerer faith in you. I praise you for all you have done in my life and all you will do; in the name of Jesus, amen.*

### JOURNALING TOGETHER

Although it is certainly possible to be a "good" person without having Jesus in your life, it's certainly easier *with* him. Spend some time journaling today about the ways in which Jesus guides your path. Use one, two, or more of the prompts below to get you started.

Describe your life before Jesus.

Describe your life after Jesus.

Does having the God of Love residing in your heart make it easier or harder to "do the right thing"?

# 2 Timothy

Many biblical scholars believe this letter, written in or about 60 A.D., from the apostle Paul to his young protégé, Timothy, may have been his very last correspondence before he was martyred in Rome. Facing the end of his days, Paul allows some of his deepest feelings to emerge on paper. He talks about God's faithfulness, forgiveness, and unending love. He talks about Timothy's contributions to his missionary purposes, and he spends a little time advising the young man on the future. The ultimate message of this letter is to remind Timothy God is always in control.

# *Their Legacy*

*[5]I have been reminded of your sincere faith, which first lived in your grandmother Lois and in your mother Eunice and, I am persuaded, now lives in you also. —2 Timothy 1:5*

There was a time right after the birth of our youngest daughter when my husband and I lived with my grandmother, for a while. Our daughter had been born with several life-threatening congenital issues that kept her confined to an incubator in the hospital long after I had been released. Since our own home was far from the hospital and my grandmother lived close to it, she invited us and our other two children to stay in her guest room for a while. As we spent time with our newborn daughter each day in the neonatal intensive care unit, our two older children stayed home with "Meemaw."

One afternoon when my husband and I came back from visiting the baby, we found the two older kids (who were eight and five) sitting on the front porch in Meemaw's lap. She was speaking softly as we approached, and was pointing to something at the other end of the porch. I heard her say, "I pray for him every morning because I know God sends him here to check on me." I turned and looked in the direction she was pointing, and was startled to see a large, 18-inch lizard sunning itself on her banister. I was stunned. My grandmother was deathly afraid of creepy crawly things like lizards.

I waited until the children had gone into the house with their father before saying, "I have two questions. First, why is it you run screaming like a banshee from skinks no bigger than your smallest finger, but seem so unafraid of that behemoth over there? Second, why in the world would you pray for it?"

She broke into a grin and explained that skinks, geckos and other small creatures frightened her because they tended to drop off the ceiling and fall into her hair. "I can't abide that kind of sneaky behavior from any living creature."

She went on, "But this one and I have an agreement. As long as he sits over there on the railing where I can keep an eye on him, I won't chase after him with a broom."

I laughed as I asked, "What did you mean when you told the kids you prayed for it every day? It's just a lizard."

She sat still for minute and thought before she answered. "Well, I may not like spiders or mice. And, I sure don't like snakes or toads. But, God made them. I'm assuming He had good reasons. And, as long as *this* lizard continues to be a gentleman, I'm willing to pray every day he doesn't end up under the tires of the neighbor's Ford. Of course, if that's God's will...."

My grandmother passed into God's Kingdom in July 2001. I will always miss her charming country wit and sunny smile. What I often miss, even more, is the knowledge that as long as she was alive she was praying for me—and the lizard, *apparently*—every day.

Of all the things we can pass down to the generations who follow us, our faith is the most precious. Neither the finest china nor the shiniest set of polished silver can compare. No family heirloom can be counted as valuable.

When our children see us pray, watch us worship; hear us quote the words of Christ, and see us standing on the promises of God, their feet are firmly planted in both their heritage and their future. By sharing our faith in action, we are showing its value in our own lives, and how precious it should be in theirs.

Our children are our greatest blessings. They are also our greatest responsibilities. They belonged to God first and they will be His again, some day. In the in-between, we are charged with their care. It is our spiritual duty, and it should be our personal joy, to share our love of Christ with them. There should be no higher priority in our lives.

I would encourage you to dedicate each day to building your children's faith, even if they're grown and have children of their own. Pray daily for them. Share the stories of God's miracles in your life. Show them God's character at work in you—demonstrate forgiveness, love, charitable giving, and respect for all others. Anoint them with His blessings.

In all you do, show God in you.

### PRAYING TOGETHER

*Father, I pray today with sweet joy in my heart. I would ask of you one simple but powerful thing: let my words change at least one family, today. Open the eyes of at least one woman. Make her aware that no matter how deeply personal and private her relationship with you may be, her faith in you should be visible in all she says and does. Her children should see Jesus every time they see her. Help her to remember the most precious gift*

*she could ever give them is the priceless gift of you.*
*I pray in Jesus' name, amen.*

### *JOURNALING YOUR THOUGHTS*

I read somewhere that children are video cameras with legs. They watch and emulate everything we do. Like our eye color and skin tone, we pass our beliefs and character on to them whether we are actively aware of the transfer or not. What are you passing on to your children?

What things are the children in your life watching you do? (For example: Praying, Praising, Worshiping, Cursing, Lying, Cheating) Make an honest list.

Of the things you've seen your children do, after watching you do the same, how many make you proud?

Is there something (or many things) you need to change?

# Titus

A Gentile convert and contemporary of the Apostle Paul, Titus could easily be called a company man, a true servant of the church. He went where he was needed, when he was needed, and he always delivered. On the Island of Crete, Titus was assigned to solve the divisions, differences, and strife running rampant in the church there. This epistle, from Paul to Titus, includes detailed instructions for structuring the church and choosing elders. It also contains some edifying encouragement for both Titus and the rest of us.

# In Chains

*[7]...so that, having been justified by his grace, we might become heirs having the hope of eternal life.*
*—Titus 3:7*

My entire family is crazy about the Food Network. We gather three or four times a week to watch our favorite shows together. My husband and I are especially partial to *The Great Food Truck*

*Race* and *Diners, Drive-ins and Dives*. One favorite, a show we all enjoy is *Chopped*.

Fast-paced and sometimes wild, *Chopped* is a cooking competition in which four chefs are asked to create a unique *and edible* three course meal from some of the most extraordinary culinary combinations available. Take, for example, salmon, peanut-butter and yak's milk, or milk chocolate, pineapple and Monkfish. Yuk!

The competition is divided into three rounds (appetizer, main course and dessert). At the end of each round, those chefs who miss the mark with their dishes are—*you guessed it*—chopped.

On a recent episode one of the contestants freely admitted to having once made a big mistake in life, which resulted in a legal conviction and five years in the state penitentiary. He had only been out of prison for a short while when picked to participate on *Chopped*.

He told the cameras about the difficulty he was having finding a job. Even though he'd once been an executive chef in the past, he couldn't even get hired as a dishwasher in the present because of his ex-convict status. No one is willing to take a chance on him, to forgive him of his past. He hoped, he told the cameras, his appearance on Chopped would showcase his skills and impress someone in the viewing audience who would then offer him a job.

Let's be honest. His chance at getting that big break is a slim one. Society can be very unforgiving towards those who make these kinds of mistakes.

How different it is with God! We are all guilty of crimes against Him; we sin daily in big and small ways and yet, He forgives.

> [12] *...as far as the east is from the west, so far has He removed our transgressions from us.*
> *—Psalm 103:12*

You might think it can't get better than that. And yet, it does! Not only does God forgive, not only does He break the chains that bind us, He goes one step further. He gives us that big break we need and makes us heirs right alongside his son, Jesus— *he who is without sin.* We're given salvation and life eternal—not because we earned it, but because

He gives it through grace! This whole concept is just beyond amazing to me! It makes me want to end every sentence with an exclamation point! I just get so excited!

If you're worrying about your past coming between you and God, well…don't. Why would you put yourself in chains like that? If you've truly repented, if you've asked for forgiveness from the bottom of your heart, I promise you, He gives it. You are His heir, his daughter, His child, justified by faith. Your past is in the past. Believe it. I do!

### *PRAYING TOGETHER*

*Dear Heavenly Father, I'm so excited. Just thinking about your generous Spirit and the forgiveness you give to truly repentant hearts is exhilarating. It's amazing! You are God and capable of so much more than we could ever imagine—even true forgiveness. How blessed I am to be your daughter. I pray in the name of Jesus, amen.*

### *JOURNALING YOUR THOUGHTS*

I have to admit, I've often resisted the idea that God could truly forgive and forget my sins because I have sometimes had a hard time forgiving others of even the smallest trespass. Like you, perhaps, I put my God in a box—a human-shaped box with limitations. One question I have asked of myself is: If I can't forgive so-and-so for what they've done to me, how can God ever forgive me for what I've done to Him? Do you, too, put God in a box? If so, it's time to let Him out! Use the prompts below (all or some) to journal your thoughts on this subject.

Have I placed God in a box of my own making? Have I judged Him by human standards? How so?

How does limiting God in this fashion affect my relationship with Him?

If God can forgive me, why can't I forgive myself?

# Philemon

Onesimus, the run-away slave of Philemon, a Christian believer living in Colosse, became a believer himself after hearing Paul preach the gospel in Rome. Paul writes this letter to Philemon encouraging him to welcome back his brother in Christ not as a slave but as a friend and fellow believer.

# It Only Takes a Spark

*[6]"I pray that you may be active in sharing your faith, so that you will have a full understanding of every good thing we have in Christ."*
*—Philemon 1:6*

After our daughter, Baylie, met David, she began to "gush." According to Baylie, David was fun! David was cute! David was smart! David was sensitive, amazing, funny, deep, etcetera, etcetera. She talked about him at the dinner table and during movies, TV shows and conversations about other things. She talked about him in her sleep. When they had their first fight, we heard all about it. When they made up, we heard about that, too. When he stubbed his toe, cracked his knuckles or sneezed—we got the memo. She was just so enamored with him; she could not stop talking about him. It was a very good thing we all liked him so much or we would have been sick of him very quickly.

Falling in love is an amazing experience. It fills your belly with butterflies, your head with dreams, and your heart with such powerful emotions, they can't be described *or contained.* It is such an incredible experience you have to share it with everyone you encounter.

As I write this devotional, Lester and I were preparing to celebrate our thirty-sixth wedding anniversary. Although I no longer gush about him like I used to, I do still talk about what a wonderful man he is. I do tell people what a brilliant husband, father and grandfather he is. I still talk about his heart, his character and his faith. The more I talk about him, the more others want to meet him.

It works the same wonderful way with Jesus. When He first comes into our lives, we are so full of amazement and wonder at what He did for us, we just can't help ourselves—we just have to "gush." We talk about His miracles, His Message, and His sacrifice. What He did for us is so unbelievable and awe-inspiring we are compelled to share a spark of our enthusiasm with everyone we meet. Often, we are blessed when that spark grows into a full blaze and they, too, are consumed with Him.

Over time, however, the fire within us begins to change. As we grow into our relationship with Jesus, as we begin to focus more on who He is—in addition to what He did for us—the fire in our hearts begins to burn deeper, hotter, and brighter. Its glow begins to show on our faces. Its warmth begins to spread to those around us, and others are drawn in to it, like moths to a flame. People want to meet the man who gives us that flush!

Each time we share our feelings for Jesus with others, we gain a better appreciation of him in our hearts. Paul understood that. He wrote,

> *"I pray that you may be active in sharing your faith, so that you will have a full*

*understanding of every good thing we have in Christ." –Philemon 1:6*

Paul knew each time we share our love of Jesus with someone else we're reminded of why we love Him—talking about Him fans the flame in our hearts for Him!

Share your love of Christ with another today—Start a fire that can't be stopped!

### PRAYING TOGETHER

*Father, you are the fire that warms our hearts and our Spirits. What you have given, what you have blessed us with is an eternal flame of faith and blessing. We are so grateful! Lord, give us the desire and the courage to go out among those still in the cold to spread your Word and your Message. We pray these things with the hope you will use us to bring glory to your name! We pray in the name of your Son, Jesus Christ. Amen*

### JOURNALING YOUR THOUGHTS

With every telling of our testimony, we mature and appreciate more of what we have in

Jesus. Use one or more of the suggestions below to get started applying God's principle: Sharing your faith is a wonderful way to come to a deeper and richer appreciation of what Christ can do in and to your life!

Make a commitment to yourself and God that you will engage in one act of evangelism this week—and follow through! Find a way to share your faith with at least one other person. Journal the results!

Pray that He will open the hearts and ears of those you may choose to share with. Pray God will give you the words to say and the will to say them. Pray He gives you the opportunity to trust in Him— an opportunity to share your faith with others. Pray with a real desire to make a difference. Journal the results!

# Hebrews

This letter, written to the Christian Jews of the first century, has a simple message: Out with the old and in with the new! Although many first generation Christians were raised in the Jewish faith, the unknown author of the book of Hebrews makes it clear to them the old rituals, laws, and sacrifices were no longer necessary. Jesus became the final sacrifice when he died on the cross. His death and subsequent resurrection signaled the beginning of a *new* contract with God and a *new* beginning. The author of Hebrews urged his readers to have faith, patience, and to trust God.

# Waiting for an Answer

*36Patient endurance is what you need now, so that you will continue to do God's will. Then you will receive all that he has promised.*
*—Hebrews 10:36*

Can I be perfectly honest with you? I have many, *many* faults. There are too many to list, truthfully. But I will tell you that I talk too fast, too much, and I tend to ramble. Plus, I have a deeply seated need to be right—*all the time.* And, as hard as it may be to believe, I've been told I have an over-inflated sense of my own "funny factor." (*Now* you're smiling...aren't you?) These things are fixable but the one fault I cannot seem to overcome is my lack of patience.

It's a fast-paced, on-demand, multi-tasking, get-it-now kind of a world and I like it that way. I fit right in! I don't have time to wait on the things I want and need. The way I see it, I should be able to lose twenty pounds in twenty minutes. I should be able to grow long healthy nails in the snap of a finger. I should be able to shop online at three in the morning, in my PJs, and have my purchase arrive within the hour. Is that really too much to ask?

Sometimes we Christians think of God in this same way, as a provider of drive-thru phenomenon and wonders. We pray our requests and concerns and wait *impatiently* for service, tapping our toes and banging our fists on our Bibles shouting out to God, *"Excuse me! I ordered a miracle a minute ago and I haven't gotten it yet. What seems to be the problem?"* The problem is…it doesn't work that way.

Today's passage in Hebrews begins with the phrase "patient endurance." Did you know that same phrase is repeated seven times in the book of Revelation? That's not all. Peter uses it several times in his epistles. Paul, too, encourages his readers to practice patient endurance in the book of Romans. James does the same in his letter, and the phrase is seen many times in the books of Colossians, 2 Thessalonians, 1 & 2 Corinthians, and so on, and so on.

Do you know why so many New Testament Biblical authors called upon their readers to be patient and endure their circumstance? Because, long before microwaves, airplanes and fast-food drive-thru windows, first-century Christians were in just as much of a hurry for God to answer their prayers as we are now. However, they received their answers in the same way we do—in *God's* time.

It isn't easy to be patient or to endure our circumstances while we wait for God to answer our prayers. What we have to remember is sometimes God's silence *is* an answer in and of itself. It means "not now" or "just wait."

He sees things we can't see. He knows things we don't know. We have to believe His plan is to prosper us and not harm us (Jeremiah 29:11). We have to trust!

I once asked God for a new (to me) car a neighbor was selling. God did not answer me, and provided no way for me to buy the car. It sold to another neighbor. I was so disappointed. However, it later turned out the car needed a whole new brake system. The neighbor who bought the car could afford to replace the old system, but I couldn't have. In the beginning, God's silence upset me. Eventually, though, I realized He was doing what was best *for me*.

Don't rush to assume God is ignoring you or making you wait in your circumstance to punish or be cruel to you. God would never do any of those things! He loves you. He asks you to be patient for reasons you can't always comprehend. Continue to do God's will...be patient and endure...

*Then you will receive all that He has promised*
*—Hebrews 10:36.*

You can count on it!

### PRAYING TOGETHER

*Father, Abba, it is so hard sometimes to be patient and endure. Like children, we want what we want when we want it and don't often understand why you make us wait. Give us the strength and ability to be patient and endure. Give us peace in our circumstances and the wisdom to know you are moving in our lives whether we realize it or not. Help us to accept your answers even if they aren't what we want to hear—even if your answer is silence. We pray all these things in the name of your Son, Jesus. Amen.*

### JOURNALING YOUR THOUGHTS

Are you familiar with the phrase "God moves in mysterious ways"? What does that mean to you? Have you ever considered that even when God is not moving—when he's being perfectly still and silent—that, *in itself*, is sometimes an answer to prayer?

Think of a time when you may have imagined God was ignoring you, not answering your prayers. In hindsight, can you think of a way He may have answered after all? Write about it in your journal.

Garth Brooks sings a song called "Unanswered Prayers." Some of the lyrics are: *...just because He doesn't answer doesn't mean He don't (sic) care. Some of God's greatest gifts are unanswered prayers"*. Choose a memory of an unanswered prayer in your life. How would your life have turned out if God had answered the way you wanted Him to at the time? Journal your thoughts.

# James

Written by the purported younger brother of Jesus, the book of James is literally an instruction booklet for Christian living. James addresses different vices Christians may be faced with each day—lust, pride, envy and greed—and gives practical solutions on how to face them. He answers the question, "What would Jesus do?"

---

# Just a Man

*[17]"Elijah was a man just like us. He prayed earnestly that it would not rain, and it did not rain on the land for three and a half years. [18]Again he prayed, and the heavens gave rain, and the earth produced its crops." —James 5:17-18*

Several years ago, a good friend's husband came down with pneumonia and had to be admitted to the hospital. I got a call from a member of our prayer chain who asked me to pray for him *"in a hurry."* Of course, I did.

Afterwards, I found myself at my computer praying again in the form of an email to the sick man's wife. I told her how God had moved me to continue praying for him until the crisis was over. Then, I opened up a word processing program on my computer and poured out my prayers on "paper." I didn't leave my keyboard for the next hour. I continued to pray over the next several days, because God moved me to do so.

It wasn't long before we all got the good news. Tim was on the road to recovery, and would soon be allowed to leave the hospital. Marie, Tim's wife, sent a personal thank-you note to each of us on the prayer chain for our efforts on his behalf. To me Marie wrote, "Although I know everyone in our group was praying, I really felt *you* went the extra mile. I could actually feel your prayers covering us. I think it's because of *you* Tim recovered."

I was secretly tickled she thought so (everyone wants to believe they can make a difference in someone else's life). However, my mother's lessons on humility immediately kicked in. I wrote back to Marie and reminded her I was part of a group of prayer warriors. *"My prayers alone could never make such a big difference."* However, I've since discovered, by reading the book of James, they can! And so can yours.

Though my mother was always wise to remind me not to let my head swell—to remember God alone can bring about miracles—it is also wise to remember

*"the effective, fervent prayer of a righteous man avails much."* —James 5:16

I am not an evangelist, pastor, or prophet. I cannot sing like an angel or preach to the multitudes. I can, however, pray. James tells us in today's passage that Elijah was a man just like us. Although he *was* a prophet, a preacher, and chosen by God to do great things, he was also just a man. Yet when he prayed, God listened. God listens to you and me, as well. In the book of Isaiah, God says,

*"Before they call I will answer; while they are still speaking I will hear."* —Isaiah 65:24

Whenever you are tempted to believe you are too small or too insignificant to make a difference, remember this: Moses and David were just shepherds; Daniel was just a slave; Peter was just a fisherman, and Paul was just a lawyer. Yet each of them trusted in the Lord with all they were. Their faith was strong. You may be just a mom, just an employee, just a teacher or the just the president of a company, but if your faith is strong, you can move mountains! The truth is you're not *just* anything…you're a child of God! That makes you incredibly important and amazingly powerful if you believe!

[20] *"And Jesus said unto them…for verily I say unto you, if you have faith as a grain of mustard seed, you shall say unto this mountain, remove from here to yonder place; and it shall remove; and nothing shall be impossible unto you."*
—*Matthew 17:20*
**(King James 2000 Bible)**

## *PRAYING TOGETHER*

*Oh Father, how we love you and praise you! What a blessing it is to know that through Jesus' actions on the cross, because of His sacrifice, we are no longer separated from you by sin. We can have a personal, intimate, loving relationship with you, through prayer. We can bring to you whatever is in our hearts—joy, despair, worry or questions— and you will hear us when we call! We ask you to lead us toward a stronger, more faithful prayer relationship with you and teach us as we go that even with faith as small as a mustard seed we can move mountains! In Jesus' name we pray, amen.*

## *JOURNALING YOUR THOUGHTS*

Like the muscles in our bodies, our faith and prayer muscles must be exercised to grow big and strong. Think about the state of your spiritual physique. Is it strong and sturdy or flabby and weak?

How often do you pray? Is it enough? Why or why not?

# 1 Peter

The apostle Peter wrote this letter to the Christians living in the land of Asia Minor. The church there was suffering horrible persecution. Some of the believers, frightened and tormented, were considering reverting back to the Jewish faith to escape the hostilities they faced daily for their belief in Christ. Peter sought to encourage them, and give them practical advice for triumph in the face of adversity. He encouraged them to lean on one another for support, trust God, and resist the pull of Satan. Through this letter, Peter turned their eyes toward their goal of eternity with Jesus.

---

# *The King of the Jungle?*

*[8]"The devil prowls around like a roaring lion, looking for someone to devour. [9]Resist him..."*
*—1 Peter 5:8-9*

Like any cat, the African lion is most successful at filling his stomach when he hides from and silently stalks his prey rather than trying to run it down. Most lions are incredibly slow runners compared to their prey. Even at top speed, they can barely reach 31 mph (and only for very short distances). Conversely, gazelles and antelopes can reach speeds of up to 44 mph, wildebeests can manage a whopping 49 mph, and fat little warthogs can run as fast as 35 mph. There is such a huge difference between the sprinting skills of a lion and its prey that most prey animals don't even bother to hit full speed when running away. How embarrassing for the lions!

Since they can't outrun their prey, lions have to outwit them. Most often, instead of chasing after their meals, they stalk from cover to cover, tree to bush, getting as close to their prey as they dare before pouncing and catching their dinner unaware. They have been known to climb trees and rock outcroppings, to drop down on inattentive animals from above. Occasionally, they simply walk into the middle of a field of tall grass and plop down, as if to nap, while all the while lazily waiting for some unsuspecting wildebeest or zebra to drop by for a quick meal. Even when using these different strategies, the lion is most successful when he catches his victim all alone—away from the herd.

The devil hunts in a very similar manner.

It's hard for me to imagine Satan prowling after or stalking victims while hoofing it up and down the aisles of my church. Nor can I envision him hiding beneath the tables during my Bible study meetings. However, when I'm all alone, in the chaos of my mind, I know the devil is waiting there, crouched behind a fear, ready to pounce.

We are at our most vulnerable when we are mentally and emotionally alone. When we stop trusting God; when we give up on prayer; when we are anxious or stressed about things we cannot change; when we divorce ourselves from our church families and turn our backs on Jesus, that's when the devil closes in. Fear, concern, apprehension, distrust, disquiet, dread, alarm… these are some of the disguises the devil uses to sneak up on us and tear us apart.

We must keep Peter's warning in the forefront of our minds,

*"The devil prowls around like a roaring lion,*
*looking for someone to devour. Resist him..."*
—*1 Peter 5:8*

We must remember God never leaves us. He walks the aisles of our church, sings in our choir, and sits next to us in Bible study. He is there in the sermon, scripture, and prayer. He is also in the arms of our family and the hearts of our friends. He is beside us on the couch as we watch TV, and He kneels by our beds as we sleep. He is with us even in the chaos of our own minds. Although we may allow ourselves to *feel* alone, we never truly are.

Be ever vigilant against the enemy. Do not fear the roar of the hungry lion. You are never alone and you are never in danger when you remember that God is near.

### *PRAYING TOGETHER*

*Lord, I raise my face to your glory. I praise your name and thank you, God, for being ever-present in my life. I pray you will remind me always I have nothing to fear when you are with me. No hungry lion or shameful sin can devour me when you are my champion. I pray my gratefulness in the name of Jesus, amen.*

### *JOURNALING YOUR THOUGHTS*

There are times when we all *feel* alone. However, God tells us, "I will never leave you nor forsake you" (Hebrews 13:5 NIV). What a joy it is to carry around that promise in your heart! Use one or more of the prompts below to journal about your feelings in this area.

Complete this thought: I remember a time I felt all alone and _____.

Did God ease your fears? Why or why not?

If not, what or *who* do you think prevented Him from helping you?

What could *you* have done to help Him help you?

# 2 Peter

Written in or around 66 AD, the apostle Peter authored this epistle shortly before his crucifixion in Rome. It is a letter of encouragement towards spiritual growth, and a call to arms for all believers. Peter warns of false teachers and their doctrines, which war against the Gospel and the teachings of the church. It is, Peter wrote, up to believers to fight against heresy and believe only the truth—Jesus *will* return someday, bringing order to a disorderly world, peace to chaos, and light to darkness.

# Liars and Con-men and Cheats! Oh, My!

*[1]But there were also false prophets among the people, just as there will be false teachers among you. They will secretly introduce destructive heresies, even denying the sovereign Lord who bought them—bringing swift destruction on themselves. —2 Peter 2:1*

Deidre was my neighbor for a while. She was a lovely, soft-spoken and gentle lady—a woman who loved the Lord—engendering only kindness and tenderness from those who knew her. Deidre's husband, on the other hand, was anything but gentle or kind. He was brutish, obnoxious, and crude. He seized every opportunity to embarrass, hurt, and humiliate Deidre and their three sons.

One morning, as she and I stood in our front yards talking, she broke down and cried, begging for my forgiveness. During the evening before, her husband had been quite surly and overtly rude to my husband and me over the subject of property lines. She was completely humiliated and embarrassed by his behavior and tone.

As we talked, I blurted out the question that had been on my mind for years, "What did you ever see in that man?" I clapped my hands over my mouth when I realized I'd actually spoken them out loud. Suddenly, I was the one who was embarrassed. Yet, she didn't seem to mind the question at all. She thought for a moment and answered slowly. "I think," She said, "I let him sell me a bill of goods. He made me believe the lie."

On occasion we are all taken in by the liars of this world. We fall for scams and cheats; we listen to liars and loons. We subvert our good instincts and gut reactions and go with the crowd or, leave behind good sense to take a road less traveled—always with the same result—heartbreak and failure.

Peter warned us this would happen. He told us there would be false teachers and leaders among us who would not have our best interest at heart. These teachers would challenge our right thinking and sabotage our relationship with the Lord. Peter warns they will mix truth with falsehood in order to lure us in, like fishermen baiting a hook. Once "hooked," it will be too late for us.

Although Peter's epistle was written to the believers of his own time, he seemed to have a unique perspective reaching across the centuries to us today. It is so easy to become enamored with charismatic, energetic, and exciting speakers and evangelists. They smile their winning smiles and preach so eloquently from God's Word. We are won over by their personalities and pretty words.

Yet, it is their actions of which we should be more aware.

The man who preaches personal poverty is often counted among the wealthiest. The one who postulates the importance of chastity is often guilty of adultery. Those who sermonize on the value of truth are sometimes the biggest liars—all in the name of God.

You may wonder; how can I tell the difference between a true disciple and a false teacher? The answer is simple. Know the character of God. Read His Word. Know His thoughts. Listen for His still small voice. The Holy Spirit lives within your heart, so turn inward to hear what He has to say and pray, pray, pray!

If anything you see, hear, or are taught interferes with or goes against the Word of God, then it is wrong. Did you know that even Paul was not above examination in his teachings?

*[11]Now the Berean Jews were of more noble character than those in Thessalonica, for they received the message with great eagerness and*

*examined the Scriptures every day to see if what
Paul said was true. —Acts 17:11*

You cannot be led astray if you know the
Lord in your own heart! Stand firm on the promises
of God. Live righteously. Love God. It's just that
easy.

### PRAYING TOGETHER

*Father, what a frightening and scary world
we live in today when we know we can't always
trust those around us, even those who claim to come
from you. We ask you to open our eyes and hearts to
deceivers. Let us see them for who they really are,
long before they can harm our relationship with
you. Give us each a discerning spirit and a
willingness to cling to your Word only. We pray in
the name of Jesus, the most trusted one. Amen.*

### JOURNALING YOUR THOUGHTS

We've all been lied to; we've been scammed
and cheated and hurt. These are the hazards of
living in a secular world. Use today's journaling
time to explore your thoughts on the subject.

Employ one, two or all of the prompts to help get you started.

I was lied to when _____.
Write a narrative about this incident. Be sure to include how you felt about the deception, how it concluded and whether or not you turned to God for help.

Find a scripture which might help you to remember to test all teaching, so you can't be led astray in the future.

Here are some of the ones I might use:
*Proverbs 3:5, Galatians 1:8-9, 1 Corinthians 4:6, Proverbs 15:4.*

Using your scripture as your starting point,
examine your life. Is there any place in which you
may be under the influence of a false teacher now?

# 1 John

The apostle John had a special love for the readers of this epistle—believers in Christ Jesus. He calls them his "little children," and instructed them in the ways of Christian living as a father might. He encouraged them to hold strong to their faith, be examples of loving forgiveness when dealing with non-believers; be the light in a dark world, and to always remember the glories of heaven wait for those who believe!

## *Turn Your Eyes upon Jesus*

*[17]The world and its desires pass away, but the man who does the will of God lives forever.*
*—1 John 2:17*

Our son, Jonathan, purchased his very first laptop computer with his very first paycheck. It was a midnight black 15.6" HP Pavillion laptop with a black-lit flat-screen monitor and an AMD Radeon

7660 GB graphic card (whatever that means); and, it came with 6 GB of memory and a 640 GB hard drive (whatever *that* means).

As Jonathan listed each of the dozen or so features, including built-in high speed wireless and web cam, his smile grew bigger. "I can play DVDs on this thing, listen to music, watch TV online, and play HD games."

I asked, "So does this mean you're going to get rid of the TV, the PlayStation, the iPod and all the other gadgets you have in this room?" The look he shot in my direction made me feel as if I'd just asked something really stupid.

"*Nooo*," he grumbled, "Actually, I finally have all the stuff I've ever wanted. I'm in heaven!"

Unfortunately, we live in a world in which, for some, the accumulation of *stuff* truly is the definition of paradise. But sadly, for these, there never seems to be enough stuff. There is always something bigger, bolder, brighter, better; the shiny new toy of today is yesterday's news, tomorrow.

Most of us, however, know the important things in life aren't *things* at all. But, instead, are the relationships we have with others. And, the most important relationship of all is the one we have with God. Or, should I say, the relationship we <u>should</u> have with God.

Don't let the *stuff* in your life get between you and Him. Turn off that cell phone! Put away the iPod and step away from your computer. Spend some time today worshipping the King. Talk to Him; *listen* to Him. Study His Word. These are the ways to really get to know Him. By doing these things, you will be following the Will of God.

It's not that hard. You did the same with your husband or boyfriend, right? Didn't you spend time with your friends this way, too, in order to get to know them? You went out, you had lunch and talked. You asked questions. You told stories about your life and listened to stories from them. That's how relationships are formed. It works the same with God, but only if you give Him your full attention.

Remember, all those things we tend to accumulate are still just *things*. They can't love you. They can't hold, comfort, or listen to you when you hurt. They won't laugh with you or keep your secrets. God will do all those things and more if only you give Him half of a chance. Turn your eyes upon Jesus today and let everything else fall away.

*Turn your eyes upon Jesus,*
*Look full in His wonderful face,*
*And the things of earth will grow strangely dim,*
*In the light of His glory and grace.*

**Turn Your Eyes Upon Jesus**
**—Helen Howarth Lemmel**

(Read Mark 10:17-31 for extra insight)

### *PRAYING TOGETHER*

*Today, Father, I will turn my eyes upon Jesus and let everything else fade away...*

### *JOURNALING YOUR THOUGHTS*

Our hearts and minds are often clogged with static—TV's blare, iPods and stereos blast, computers buzz, cell phones beep—this is the white noise of the world we live in. For today's exercise, take some time to *listen* to God. Turn off your devices. Close your doors and sit silent. Wait upon the voice of the Lord. What will He have for you today? Use one or more of the prompts below to journal your discoveries.

Today, it was (or was not) easy to sit silent and wait upon the Lord because

_____

_____

The message I received from God was

_____

How will this affect my life?

# 2 John

This second epistle of John contains only 303 words (four more than the third letter of John), making it *almost* the shortest book of the Bible. It is addressed: "To the lady chosen by God and to her children…" (Verse 1) Although some believe John's letter may have been written to or for one special lady in his life, most believe instead it was written to a particular church, the "lady" being the church, her "children" being the believers in Christ. Regardless, the letter was written as a warning against false teachings and those who would contradict the wisdom and leading of Christ. It was also written as encouragement for believers to keep their relationship with Christ close to their hearts.

# Anyway

*[12] I have much to write to you, but I do not want to use paper and ink. Instead, I hope to visit you and talk with you face to face, so that our joy may be complete.*

*—2 John 12*

Recently, one of my daughters accused me of being agoraphobic, "You never want to leave the house. You'd spend your whole life on Facebook if we'd let you." Although she was teasing, there is some validity to what she says. I am, *sometimes*, more comfortable in the cyber-world than the real one.

On Facebook I can be witty and sophisticated, urbane (but never snotty), hip (without looking stupid), and beautiful. No one in Facebook-land need know I'm sitting in front of the computer at 3 p.m. still wearing my pajamas, mismatched socks, and a baseball cap covering un-brushed hair. The point is, people in cyberspace never have to know the *real* me.

And that, of course, is where the problem lies.

Because of our busy, harried lives, we rely too much on texts, emails, instant messaging, and online conversations. And because we do, we lose the intimacy of face-to-face relationships. We lose ourselves—and others—in the anonymity of cyberspace.

Take, for example, the connection I have with my friend, Maria, who lives in Canada. I met her through Facebook several years ago. We often tease we are "sisters from different misters" because we are so much alike. We are both Christians and members of the same online prayer group. We are both writers, in love with the written word. We are both mothers and wives. I know Maria...but I don't really *know* her. Do you know what I mean?

I've never hugged Maria, or sat in her living room and looked into her eyes as she spoke from her heart. I've never eaten her cooking or laughed with her until we both cried. We've never held one another's hands to pray. We've never been silent together. I couldn't even tell you for certain how tall she is, or whether she is thin or round like me, and I don't know for sure how old she is. When it comes right down to it, I don't know Maria at all— although, I'd love to.

Even centuries ago, the apostle John knew this could be a problem. He wrote to members of a particular church—*the lady chosen by God*—and told them he would write no more than was necessary using paper and ink. Instead, he said, he would save his most important message for a time when he could see them face-to-face.

He needed to look into their eyes and speak from his heart. He needed to hold their hands and pray with them. He wanted them to hear the passion in his voice and see the joy on his face as he spoke about Jesus. He wanted them to feel his arms around them and know the love he carried in his breast for them. He wanted them to know him, to *really* know him. And, he wanted to know them just as intimately.

God feels this same way about us. It wasn't enough for Him to sit on his throne in heaven and watch us from afar. God wanted to laugh and cry with us, and touch us with hands that could heal us and comfort us. He wanted to experience us—not from an eternity away, but up close and personal. God wanted to *know* us. And so, He came. He came in the person of Jesus. GOD…yet, man. Majestic…yet, mainstream. Omnipotent …yet, ordinary.

God went to astonishing lengths to push past the boundaries of casual interest in us. He sent His Son—*He came Himself*—to live among us, to get to know us. More importantly, He gave us the opportunity to really get to know Him. He showed us His character, compassion and loving care. He shared his history and heritage, adopting us into his family. He gave us His counsel *and* His correction. Then, through the person of Jesus, God showed us just how much He cared. He allowed us to watch Him die and then conquer death. After that, with what can only be described as miraculous generosity and love, God gave *us* eternity.

No one on earth before or since has ever loved us like that!

As a child of God you are never disconnected from the Father! He knows you like no one else ever could. God loves the real you...the you in pajamas and mismatched socks; the you with anger issues and jealousies; the you with ambition and drive; the you who eats Oreos at three in the morning and cries; the you with six kids and no patience; the you who hates how she looks in jeans; the you who cheats on her taxes, her exams, her husband. He knows you! He Knows YOU!

... ... ...And He loves you *anyway*.

### *PRAYING TOGETHER*

*Dear God in heaven, tears roll down my face as I ponder the wonder of you. You know me better than anyone else, and yet, you love me anyway.* You *love* me... anyway.
*I stand amazed and pray, in the name of Jesus, Amen.*

### *JOURNALING TOGETHER*

Journaling is a tool we use to explore our innermost thoughts and feelings. On this day, I'd like you to explore (with honesty) how you feel on the subject of God's love. Despite our many faults, God loves us anyway. How does that make *YOU* feel?

The idea that God may love me, despite my many faults leaves me feeling _____

_____

Why?

# 3 John

This letter from the apostle John to a friend, Gaius, is the shortest book in the Bible (it has the fewest words; 2 John has fewer verses). Still, its message is powerful. John tells Gaius it is our duty to support other Christians—in any way we are able—as they spread the gospel of Jesus Christ. John mentions two other men in this letter, Diotrephes and Demetrius. The first he considers a bad example; the latter a good example of Christianity. He encourages Gaius to follow only what is good.

# Monkey See, Monkey Do

*[11]Dear friend, do not imitate what is evil but what is good. Anyone who does what is good is from God. Anyone who does what is evil has not seen God.*
*—3 John 11*

"Monkey see; monkey do...how long have you been a monkey"?

This is a question I asked my children a lot as they grew up. I was forever battling against the anthem of childhood, "everybody else is doing it." Don't all mothers fight this same fight? We want our kids to grow up to be unique and special. We want them to stand out and be noticed. We want them to be unicorns in a world full of simians!

Our kids, however, want to jump off the bridge because everyone else is doing it.

Even adults sometimes find it easier to "go along to get along." Have you ever been part of a gossip session, talking about things you know you shouldn't but unable to stop yourself for fear of looking uptight or stuck-up to the people you're with? I'm not proud of it, but I know I've been caught in this trap before.

It's easier, sometimes, to be a monkey than a unicorn. However, it's not always the right thing to do.

This is the message John tries to convey to Gaius in this his third epistle.

Gaius and John have mutual acquaintances, Diotrephes and Demetrius. Although as readers of this letter we have no background information on these men, it's easy to differentiate between the two. One of them impresses John…the other does not.

John describes Diotrephes as someone who "loves to be the leader" in the church. Yet, Diotrephes does not recognize the authority of the apostles. John depicts Diotrephes as wicked, unwelcoming to other Christians, and bullying to the other members of his church. John goes on to call him a "bad example" and warns Gaius not to let Diotrephes influence him.

In contrast, John hails Demetrius as someone about whom "everyone speaks highly." He encourages Gaius to follow Demetrius' example, "only what is good."

It may be easier to ape the actions of the crowd—to do what everyone else is doing—but, it isn't the *right* thing to do.

Are you someone about whom others speak highly? Or, are you the example of what not to do? Think about it. If you're not following only the good, only the true, and only the beautiful—you're on the wrong path. It's harder to be a unicorn when everyone else is swinging from trees and eating bananas. But it's worth it. Unicorns are beautiful!

### PRAYING TOGETHER

*Heavenly Father, I cannot praise you enough for creating me to be a unicorn—unique in a world full of monkeys. I pray you will give me the strength and determination to follow only what is good in this world—to do what Jesus would do in every situation. He is the example I want to follow. Thank you, Lord, for the blessings in my life. I pray in the name of our returning Savior, Jesus Christ, amen.*

### JOURNALING YOUR THOUGHTS

Now is the time to "think about it." In your journal today, explore your own character and personality. *Are* you a good example for other Christians? Or, are you the Diotrephes in your circle? Use one or more of the following prompts to answer those questions for yourself.

Whenever I am faced with a choice between "going along to get along" and walking away, I most often choose to _____

Is my answer above something I'm proud of? Why or why not?

What can I do to make it easier on myself to follow "only what is good"?

Do I really want to be unicorn? Or, am I content being a monkey?
Why?

What's wrong with being a monkey?

# Jude

This small book, a personal letter consisting of only 25 verses, was written by Jude the (possible) half-brother of Jesus. It is not known to whom he was writing. However, his passion for his subject is most clear. The apostle warns his contemporaries against the evils of false-teaching, and encourages them to stick closely to the true wisdom of Jesus, the Christ.

Jude's warning to his own people is still very relevant today. It links both the memories of past punishments for evil and the prophecy of God's future wrath against all inequity. It is a call to all believers to remain in God's truth and stay on the path of *true* righteousness.

# Crouching Tiger

*¹⁰Yet these people slander whatever they do not understand and the very things they do understand by instinct—as irrational animals do—will destroy them. —Jude 1:10*

I suppose it was inevitable, as coordinator of the very large women's mentoring ministry in our church that I would eventually come up against criticism. However, the first time such criticism was brought to my attention, it was incredibly hard to take—especially when the people doing the criticizing weren't aware I could hear their conversation.

After a very well-attended luncheon; after I'd said my official goodbyes and few more personal ones; I ran to the ladies' room down the hall and around the corner from the banquet room. As I was returning, I could hear a group of ladies, just out of my sight, having a conversation in hushed and whispered tones. Although I was not at first aware of the subject of their discussion, I found myself inexplicably slowing my pace and turning my ear in their direction, straining to hear every word. My heart began to pound.

*"I don't think she knows what's she's doing."*

*"I don't think she realizes how awful she sounds…"*

*"She's sweet, truly. But, I think she's in over her head."*

It only took a few seconds for me to realize they were speaking about me! I stood there quietly in the shadows, just a few feet from them and I listened as they oh-so-sweetly tore me to ribbons. They discussed my clothing choices, hairstyle, my Texas twang, and my choice of leadership team members. It appeared each of them felt they could do a better job than I. Fair enough. I was somewhat new in the position of coordinator and had yet, *I suppose*, proven my abilities. However, the personal attacks were not fair and had my blood boiling.

It was all I could do to hold myself back from charging into their midst like a crouching tiger, roaring my frustration and anger. Instead, I tiptoed in the opposite direction, walked out and around the building, and came back to the banquet room through a back door. Although I was seething, I went to work on the clean-up with the rest of my leadership team and kept my hurt feelings to myself. As the group of gossipers prepared to leave, they stopped to say goodbye.

*"What a lovely event, Angie!"*

*"I love to hear you speak. You should become a public orator!"*

*"This was so much fun! You and your team are so talented!"*

Can you imagine how hard it was for me to be civil? Thank the Lord He held my tongue! To have responded as I wanted to would have been both un-Christian and un-ladylike.

But let's be honest. I have been on the other side of that conversation before. Of this, I am not proud. I would wager a guess you can say the same thing. Jude warns us against this type of behavior. He tells us those who slander others, who murder like Cain; debase themselves for money and rebel against God bring about their own destruction.

As others did before him, Jude encourages believers to stand firm in their faith, to be strong in the face of evil, and keep to the path chosen for us by God. Although we are human, and therefore capable of slipping and falling, we are Christians.

We must learn to trust in Jesus, listen to His Holy Spirit guiding from our hearts, and obey.

I was blessed that day so long ago. The Holy Spirit kept me from blasting my accusers and making a fool of myself. Had I ignored Him and responded in kind to their slander and heartlessness, I would have lived up to (or should I say down to) every one of their accusations. God knew me better than that and would not allow it. He is so good to me.

He will be good to you, as well…if you allow it. Listen to His still small voice. Obey His commands. Follow where He leads and you will stand before Him blameless, someday!

### *PRAYING TOGETHER*

*Our Father, who art in Heaven, hallowed be Thy name! Lord I praise you for your mercy and grace. Thank you for leading me down the path of righteousness. I am blessed you care for me. I am blessed you know my name. Thank you for the miracles you have given in my life and all those yet to come. Forgive me for those times I've failed you. In Jesus' name, amen.*

***JOURNALING YOUR THOUGHTS***

Jude encourages us to live in such a way that God's love can bless us as we wait for our eternal life. Are you living in that manner? Is your own sin waiting, like a crouching tiger, to condemn you in front of God? Use one, some or all of the prompts below to help you answer these questions.

Are you proud of who you *in Christ*? Explain

Are you easily led astray by scoffers and slanderers?

What can you do to avoid those kinds of situations?

# Revelation

Admittedly, the book of Revelation is a very
confusing and complex book. It is filled with
illustrative detail of visions and prophecy. Its
allegorical style is mystifying and its story can be
somewhat frightening. However, there are pearls of
pure bliss buried in its pages—most having to do
with worship of God.

# The Nature of Worship

*[11]And they were shouting with a great roar,
"Salvation comes from our God who sits on the
throne and from the Lamb!"*
*—Revelation 7:11 (NLT)*

When Susie worships, she's a whirlwind. As
the music plays in the sanctuary, she throws up her
hands, shouts "Amen" and "Hallelujah", sways
from side to side, and often allows tears of joy to
slide down her face in rivulets, soaking the front of
her blouse. During the sermon, every time the
pastor makes a point she agrees with, Susie cries out

"Amen," and "All right!" During prayer time, she bobs her head up and down, sways from side to side, grips her hands together so tightly her knuckles turn white and she often weeps even as she smiles beatifically. When Susie worships—*each time she worships*—it is a life-changing occurrence.

Royce is not quite as demonstrative as Susie. Royce will not stand during worship unless the pastor specifically calls him out, *"Come on Royce. Stand up! Let's pray together."* He does not dance, sway, or even sing during songs. Yet, even though Royce may not be as exuberant as Susie, he's fully committed to his worship experience. Royce and Susie both love the Lord and worship with their whole hearts.

Wes worships God in a whole different way. His artistic talent is a God-given gift. Each of his works of art is stirring; each is an artistic homage to God's own art—nature. Wes is not a member of any church, and yet, he worships God with all that he is. Every Sunday morning, the sun comes up to find Wes setting up his easel somewhere in the wilderness. Sometimes, he paints majestic mountain scenes and sometimes he paints the calming waters of lakes and seas. Sometimes, tall stately pine trees are his models and every so often he paints birds, animals or fish, as well. He rarely shares his work with anyone. Most of the time when he's finished with a "Sunday Sermon," the paintings go into storage, never to be taken out again. They are each visible and very personal ode to his God.

What's important about Wes' painting is that he's painting at all. Twenty-one years ago, Wes plowed his pickup truck into a telephone poll going eighty miles an hour down a country road. He'd been drinking and should never have been behind the wheel of a vehicle. Not strapped in, Wes crashed through the windshield and lay dying, twenty feet from the truck. Had a passerby not stopped when he did, Wes would be dead today.

After being in a coma for more than thirty-nine days, Wes woke up and swore he'd been with God. He told of long walks with the Lord besides mountain streams and icy lakes. He told of sitting with his Heavenly Father on the ground at the foot of a mighty oak, laughing and sharing stories of his past. He tells of walking without talking with the one person who understood his silence better than anyone else.

Back on the earthly plane, Wes stopped drinking and turned his life around. For him, the act of worship doesn't involve a church, an organ, a hymnal, or a pastor. For Wes, worship is a return to nature and the memory of his time with God.

Each of us has a different style of worship, often shaped by our personal preferences. I worship more like Susie, and my husband worships more like Royce.

Someday, our worship will come from our very souls. When we find ourselves in heaven, we will sing hosannas and wave palm branches when He walks by. We will bow at His feet. We will give Him our adoration and He will bless us, every one. My heart beats with anticipation and leaps with joy. I cannot wait!

### *PRAYING TOGETHER*

*Heavenly Father, we worship you! You are the God of gods and the King of kings. You, God are everything. Remind me to praise you, every day, and lift you up. Help me to live the life you would be*

*proud of, so that others may see you in me. I pray
these things because I believe in you. I pray in the
name of Jesus, amen.*

## JOURNALING YOUR THOUGHTS

Do you prefer hymns or contemporary praise songs? When you worship would you prefer to be alone or with others? Think about the way you worship and journal about it, today. Use the prompts below to get your journaling juices flowing.

Describe your most joyful and/or most unsatisfying worship experience.

What was it about that experience that disappointed you or moved you so?

What do you need to be able to fully worship the Lord as he deserves?

# Epilogue

The end of the story

# Even Though

*[11] for I know the plans I have for you," declares the LORD, "plans to prosper you and not to harm you, plans to give you hope and a future.*
*—Jeremiah 29:11*

Just like I have many "favorite" flavors of ice cream and dozens of favorite recipes and too many favorite songs to mention, I have many favorite scriptures. However, Jeremiah 29:11 tops my list. It will always be my *most favorite* Word from God, because it was written just for me. It's personal.

From this passage I have God's word, his personal pledge, that he has ME on his heart. He knows what he has planned for my today and my tomorrow. He plans to bless me and keep me. In addition, he has, he does and he will bring me hope and joy and happiness every day, no matter my circumstances. Even in my darkest hours he will not let me come to harm. This scripture brings me so much comfort and joy. It is my favorite.

I would imagine you have a favorite passage as well. Perhaps one of the ones I've recorded in this book has *always* been special to you. Or, maybe, herein you've found a *new* favorite. This, too, would bring me a great deal of joy.

My goal, in writing this book, was to journal my faith for my grand-daughter. In so doing, I've shared it also with you. What I pray, more than anything else, is that at least one of the 66 scriptures I've shared—and it's corresponding story—touched your heart and brought you closer to the Lord. I pray, too, that you will share your story with others as well. You don't have to write a book. You don't have to become a world-wide speaker or evangelist. All you have to do is sit down with one person and share your testimony. That's all it takes to be prosperous in God's kingdom. Don't worry about being perfect. You're not. *But, He is*. And, even though you (and I) will never measure up—even though you will always be impractical, impatient, impulsive and *imperfect*—you can still make a difference in His story. He has plans for _you_. He

can prosper _you_. He will bless _you_. He loves..._**you**_...even though.

www.ingramcontent.com/pod-product-compliance
Lightning Source LLC
Chambersburg PA
CBHW051937090426
42741CB00008B/1180